Discovery Guide to

Zimbabwe

by Melissa Shales

IMMEL
Publishing

For my parents
with my love and thanks for introducing me to Africa

Discovery Guide to Zimbabwe, second edition
Text © 1993 by Melissa Shales

Photographs by Melissa Shales (Great Zimbabwe royal quarters, Kariba Dam, Kyle Lake, Great Zimbabwe cone-tower), Christine Osborne (Harare buses, rural housing, Harare panorama, Victoria Falls), Juliet Highet (crochet lace) and the Zimbabwe Tourist Board.

Cover design by Colin Elgie

Typeset in 10/12pt Palatino and printed in Great Britain at the Bath Press, Lower Bristol Road, Bath BA2 3BL

Published by Immel Publishing, 20 Berkeley Street, Berkeley Square, London W1X 5AE, England. Tel: 071-491 1799. Fax: 071-493 5524

ISBN 0 907151 72 8

CONTENTS

Discovery Guides   6

Introduction   7

Section 1: Background   9
  Practical Background   10
  Wildlife Background   43
  Historical Background   63
  Zimbabwe Today Background   97

Section 2: Mashonaland   105
  Harare and Environs   106
  Lake McIlwaine   119
  Chinhoyi Caves   121

Section 3: Along the Zambezi   123
  Mana Pools   124
  Kariba   128
  Lake Kariba   136
  Victoria Falls   139
  Hwange National Park   152

Section 4: Matabeleland and the South   156
  Bulawayo and Environs   157
  Khami Ruins   166
  Matobo National Park   169
  Masvingo and Environs   175
  Kyle Dam and Lake   179
  Great Zimbabwe   182
  Gonarezhou National Park   191

Section 5: The Eastern Highlands   193
  Mutare   194
  The Vumba   202
  The Nyanga   204
  The Chimanimani   211

Section 6: Appendix   214
  Language: Useful Words and Phrases   215
  Old and New Place Names   218
  Customs Allowances   220
  Some Zimbabwe Embassies and Tourist
    Offices Abroad   221
  Some Foreign Embassies in Zimbabwe   223
  Tour Companies, Car Hire and Accom-
    modation Central Booking Offices
    in Zimbabwe   225

Index   228

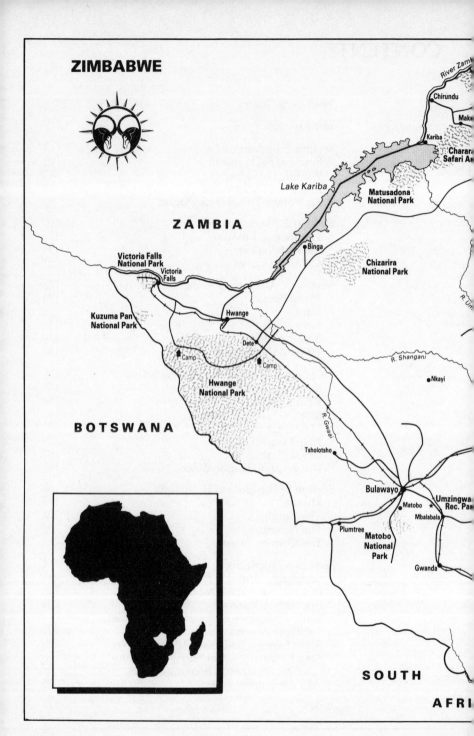

ZIMBABWE

ZAMBIA

River Zam

Chirundu

Mak

Kariba

Charara
Safari A

Lake Kariba

Matusadona
National Park

Binga

Chizarira
National Park

R. Un

**Victoria Falls
National Park**

Victoria
Falls

Hwange

Kuzuma Pan
National Park

Dete

R. Shangani

Camp

Camp

Nkayi

**Hwange
National Park**

BOTSWANA

R. Gwaai

Tsholotsho

Bulawayo

Matobo

Umzingwa
Rec. Pa

Mbalabala

Plumtree

**Matobo
National
Park**

Gwanda

SOUTH

AFRI

4

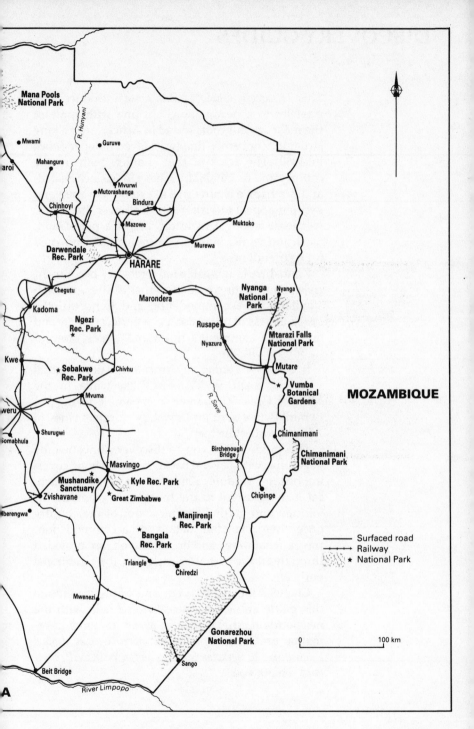

Mana Pools
National Park

Mwami

Mahangura

aroi

Guruve

R. Hunyani

Mvurwi

Mutorashanga

Chinhoyi

Bindura

Mazowe

Muktoko

Murewa

Darwendale
Rec. Park

HARARE

Chegutu

Marondera

Nyanga
National
Park

Nyanga

Kadoma

Ngezi
Rec. Park
★

Rusape

Nyazura

Mtarazi Falls
National Park
★

Kwe

★ Sebakwe
Rec. Park

Chivhu

Mvuma

Mutare

★ Vumba
Botanical
Gardens

MOZAMBIQUE

weru

Shurugwi

R. Save

omabhula

Chimanimani

Masvingo

Birchenough
Bridge

Chimanimani
National Park

Mushandike
Sanctuary ★

Kyle Rec. Park

★ Great Zimbabwe

Chipinge

Zvishavane

Mberengwa

★ Manjirenji
Rec. Park

★ Bangala
Rec. Park

Triangle

Chiredzi

Surfaced road
Railway
★ National Park

Mwenezi

Gonarezhou
National Park

0   100 km

Beit Bridge

Sango

River Limpopo

A

5

DISCOVERY GUIDES

This *Discovery Guide to Zimbabwe* introduces the traveller to a new nation, but one with some of the most ancient roots found in Africa. After a long struggle, Zimbabwe finally achieved independence in 1980. The scars of that conflict, both on the country and its inhabitants, have long since healed, and Zimbabwe is now free to extend its varied and exciting appeal to visitors from all over the world. Not least amongst its attractions is a population, black and white, living in harmony and renowned for its friendliness.

Zimbabwe is agreeable too for its lack of commercialisation, its uncrowded tourist centres, its high standards of accommodation and transport, the spaciousness of its landscape, a perfect climate and one of the continent's finest and largest concentrations of wildlife.

It possesses some of Africa's greatest natural wonders, such as Victoria Falls, while in the ruins of Great Zimbabwe, comparable to Egypt's Pyramids in extent and mystery, it offers clues to Africa's earliest history.

This guide helps you to discover Zimbabwe by beginning with several background sections covering history, wildlife, Zimbabwe today, and practical matters useful to the traveller in planning his journey and getting the most out of the country once there. Further details of accommodation, travel, what to see and do, and so on, are provided throughout the text after each city, town, national park, etc.

Changes inevitably occur and improvements to this guide are always possible. To help with the next edition, the reader is asked to send information and comments to *Discovery Guides, Immel Publishing, 20 Berkeley Street, London W1X 5AE, England*. Thank you.

INTRODUCTION

My first sight of Rhodesia was during a tropical storm of such impressive dimensions that it completely obliterated the mountainous Eastern Highlands. We had landed at Beira in Mozambique and were driving up from the coast to Umtali (Mutare) which was to be my home for the next 14 years. The little we saw was in photographic flashes as lightning lit up the bowl in the hills. It was February 1963, and I was just four. I really can't recall too much more of my first weeks in the country. What does remain is an overriding sense of colour. My memories of England were drawn in black and white, and like Dorothy, I'd been swept into a magic land of colour, the purples and crimsons of bougainvillea, the mauve and scarlet canopies of jacarandas and flame trees lining the streets in triumphal procession, the oranges of the honeysuckle and golden shower, the copper and burgundy of the young msasa leaves fiery on the hill above our house, the deep, endless blue of the sky. It was a perfect country for a child—the shoes came off, the soles of my feet hardened, I learnt to swim, I saw my first elephant and within a few months took it for granted that this was the real world. England became a rather soggy dream.

As I grew older the delights of paradise began to pall. Because Africa was all I could really remember, it held none of the romance for me that had made other writers wax lyrical. I was, I suppose, a typical teenager, far more concerned with the next party than with the great outdoors. At the same time, too, I began to realise quite what shaky foundations my easy life had been built on. Politics began to rear their head, followed soon afterwards by the very ugly reality of the war. Upset and confused and out of place, I took the easy option and the moment I left school I also left home, shaking the dust of Africa from my heels and heading back to England which had, by now, become my promised land.

Yet as so many people have said before me, Africa, once in your blood, will never let you go. Ten years later I returned to what was by now a different country—independent black Zimbabwe. It was a worrying moment. I had heard so many contradictory reports of what I might find, I wasn't at all sure it was a good idea to look back.

But as I left the airport I felt again that fizz of excitement and the blinking feeling of coming out of a tunnel as my bones warmed, flexed and filled with intense energy in the sunshine. There was an unconscious familiarity with my surroundings, but most of all I finally discovered the true appeal of Africa. The towns seemed small and slightly shabby and the shops seemed empty, but then my childhood impressions hadn't been coloured by years of living in London. Looked at objectively it was only me, not the towns, that had changed. What was different was the atmosphere. Going into the hotels and clubs and seeing relaxed, happy black faces. Ordering a drink and being welcomed to the country by people with none of the forelock-tugging servitude of the past. Everyone seemed proud of their country and its achievements, everyone was prepared to chat. I felt truly welcome, and when I told people that I had been brought up in the country I generally found myself being greeted by an all-enveloping familial bear hug, not by the suspicion I had feared.

As a child, the bush was a hot, dusty wasteland filled with ants. Now too I discovered its real glory, the subtlety of colour and texture that shaded the grass a dozen different hues of gold, the rustle of crickets and the howl of bushbabies or hyenas, the hot, sweet, sooty smell of the earth, the ability to stand alone in the evening light without seeing or hearing another human being. If at times I appear too enthusiastic, I make no apologies. I have written about Zimbabwe as I see it. It isn't perfect and I won't pretend it is, but it is enchanting, and I for one am firmly under its spell.

SECTION 1:
BACKGROUND

Practical Background

Wildlife Background

Historical Background

Zimbabwe Today Background

PRACTICAL BACKGROUND

Arrival and Departure

Air. Flying to Zimbabwe is simple with several international airlines running scheduled services to Harare including Air Zimbabwe, Zambian Airways, Kenya Airways, Ethiopian Airways, British Airways, South African Airways, Air India and Qantas. All international flights bar one are into Harare. The one exception is a flight from Johannesburg to Bulawayo and Victoria Falls. Non-stop flying time from London is about nine hours.

Flying into Harare

Overland. Zimbabwe is a landlocked country. The border with South Africa is formed by the Limpopo river, 'great, grey green and greasy, all set about with fever trees', where the elephant got his trunk in *The Just So Stories*. The northern border with Zambia is the Zambezi. There are border posts at regular points around the country, almost all served by good, tarred roads.

From Zambia...

From Zambia, you can cross in three places: the Alfred Beit Bridge leads from Livingstone to the Victoria Falls; further downstream is the Kariba Dam Wall; the main route between Lusaka and Harare crosses at Chirundu.

and from South Africa, Botswana and Mozambique

To the south are the South African border across the Limpopo at Beit Bridge, and the Kazungula and Plumtree border posts to Botswana. There are also two crossings to Mozambique at Forbes Border Post, Mutare and at Nyamapanda.

All the border posts are open from 6am to 6pm seven days a week, except Beit Bridge which remains open to 8pm.

Visas, Permits, etc. Citizens of the Commonwealth, the European Community, the USA and Canada do not require visas. South Africans do. Others should check. For a work permit, you will need to apply to the Ministry of Information. It will be harder to get the permit if you are doing a job which could be done by a Zimbabwean citizen. They are looking, as are most other countries, for specialist skills. Even then, most of the jobs available are short-term expat contracts with either charities or the government, aimed principally at training locals to take over.

Money. On entering the country you will be asked both for proof of financial support and for a return or onward ticket, or some other proof of your ability to leave again. There is no fixed minimum support level, but about £500 per person seems to be what they are looking for. A recognised credit card (American Express, Diners' Club or Mastercard/Access) is also acceptable.

You are allowed to take any amount of hard currency into the country as long as it is declared on entry, but you can only legally import or export $100 Zimbabwean. The currency declaration form you fill in on arrival will be checked on departure and you may have to provide additional proof of expenditure, so keep all receipts. Don't change too much at a time, so as not to be left trying to change Zimbabwean dollars back into hard currency at the end of your trip. It is reasonably easy to do this now, as long as your paperwork tallies, but you will always be given US dollar travellers' cheques, not cash.

Taking it with you

At the time of writing, the exchange rate was hovering around the Z$9 to £1 mark, but it tends to vary from day to day. The black market rate was up to Z$20 to £1, but penalties are severe for those who are caught. The US dollar is probably the most widely used hard currency in the country.

NB: *All dollar prices in this book are Zimbabwean dollars.*

Departure. There is a US$20 departure tax which has to be paid in hard currency. The duty-free shop at Harare Airport will happily take, and give change in, hard currency.

Prices and Inflation

This is a very rough estimate and should not be taken as gospel; the situation can change very rapidly. Food is a third of the price you would expect to pay in London. Accommodation varies dramatically in price, from about Z$60 a night at the cheaper hotels, up to about US$200 per person per night for a suite at the most expensive. Camping costs Z$6–16 per night. Car hire starts at around Z$120 a day.

Inflation is currently averaging about 20 percent a year.

Climate

Mildly tropical

Although it is firmly within the tropics, Zimbabwe's climate is rarely as grillingly hot and humid as this might suggest as it is both landlocked and fairly high. More than half the country lies above 900 metres. Unlike some tropical countries, there is even a definite winter, although it rarely gets really cold, and it never snows. Spring and autumn don't exist in a recognisable form.

The length of the days varies little between the seasons with night falling between 5.00 and 5.30 in winter and at about 7 in summer. There is no dusk as such; the light disappears, usually in a spectacular blaze, within half an hour.

Virtually all the country's rain falls in one relatively short season of heavy mid-summer storms between late November and early March. The rains bring hot, sticky nights and days covered by lowering dark clouds, constant discomfort, headaches and bad temper, only relieved by massive thunderstorms, usually in the afternoon or at night. They rarely last longer than a couple of hours, but during that time rain pounds down hard enough to hurt, and the lightning and thunder are awesome. Several people are killed by lightning each year, usually in the remote areas.

The average maximum temperature during this period is usually only in the high 20s°C, but it is only the cloud cover that brings it down this far and the high humidity makes it feel far hotter. Out of the shade, temperatures are often far higher. I once left a thermometer in a car that was standing out in the sun only to have it explode. After a storm, if the sky clears, the weather can be delightful for a while. Sadly, once the water begins to steam off the ground, it rarely takes long for the humidity to start building up again.

Zimbabweans claim that winter lasts from mid-May through to August, shiver, take to jerseys and roaring log fires. In fact the temperature is usually comparable to May/June in Britain, and is often hotter by day. This period is dry and sunny, with clear blue skies. By July the Eastern Highlands are sometimes covered with a light, drizzly mist called *guti* locally, but elsewhere the weather can be perfect, hot enough for sunbathing by day, cold enough for a fire at night.

Best seasons for visiting The best times for travelling in Zimbabwe are April/May, once the rains have finished and the temperature has come down to a level that leaves you some energy, or in September, when it is warming up again, but before the fierce dry heat of October. Be warned, however, and book ahead if you are planning to travel then as the whole country goes on holiday and many places will book up months in advance.

Local variations. Unlike Europe, the African weather varies little for hundreds, often thousands of miles. While there are obviously some variations in climate, they are not extreme. The Eastern Highlands, on the Mozambique border, are the coolest and wettest part of the country, with crisp, mountain air and nighttime frosts in winter. Mutare, however, which is in a bowl in the hills, can be as hot as the low veld, and much more humid. Matabeleland, at the other side of the country, is the driest and hottest region, bordering on the Kalahari and with little more rain than in the desert. The Hwange Plateau is noticeably cooler at night in winter than the surrounding area. On one early morning game drive in an open Land Rover, I was comfortable in a shirt, sweatshirt, jersey and a blanket—and I'm warm-blooded! But by about 10am all but the shirt had come off, and by lunchtime I was sunbathing.

Clothing

Casual cottons

Base everything on cotton, or poly-cotton mixes rather than synthetics and keep things loose for comfort in summer. The country is casual by nature, so normal day wear is cotton dresses and sandals or jeans and T-shirts. Shorts are perfectly acceptable for men, to the point where the safari suit, with long shorts and long socks, is business wear in summer although less frequently now than in the past. In winter, women add a cardigan and a pair of tights, the men go into light suits. Jackets and ties are required by the most upmarket restaurants and hotels after 4pm. Elsewhere, it is usually smart casual, although in one game park we visited, this was defined as wearing a shirt and shoes!

Theatres, concerts, etc, are still dress occasions and people will usually dress more formally for dinner parties, though long dresses are rarely worn now. Take at least one good outfit as the life is very social and it is more than likely that you will be invited out at some point during your trip.

If you are going out into the bush, take a pair of stout shoes for walking through long grass (where snakes can be a risk), a shirt with long sleeves (to ward off the evening mosquitoes) and a hat with a decent brim (to fend off the sun). Also take some sort of jacket or jumper as the temperature can fall quite dramatically at night. Choose colours that blend in if you are hoping to see animals. Most have black and white vision, but even so, brilliant colours or white have a completely different tone to the surrounding vegetation and will startle them into hiding. It is illegal for civilians to wear camouflage, and anything that looks too military is not advisable. Zimbabweans are a pretty conservative mob and anything too outrageous (by

What *not* to wear

local definition) is likely to be treated with grave suspicion.

You won't need a heavy coat, but don't forget to take a swimming costume, whatever time of year you are going.

Health

There are no statutory health requirements, but it is nevertheless advisable to have the main inoculations: yellow fever, typhoid, cholera and paratyphoid. All these diseases are present in the country, although rare. If you think you will be handling animals, also have the rabies vaccination as this is widespread amongst the local wildlife.

Inoculations and vaccinations

Aids

Aids is rife throughout the country. Avoid all unprotected (and possibly all) sexual contact and carry your own supply of sterile needles.

Malarial prophylactics are *essential*, particularly if you are going to the Zambezi Valley. A new, virulent strain of cerebral malaria has recently been found in the region, which will kill if allowed to develop, and mosquitoes are common. Always check with a tropical diseases expert as to which prophylactic you should take. Malaria is a rare disease in temperate climates and your family doctor may not be sufficiently familiar with the constant changes in prophylactics to give you the most accurate advice.

Malaria

Bilharzia, a microscopic worm carried by water snails, that attacks the liver, bowel and bladder, is present in virtually all natural water in the country. If possible, don't drink any untreated water—and don't swim in any lakes or rivers. If you can't avoid it, towel off briskly with a dry towel as soon as you are on the shore again. It takes up to 20 minutes for the worm to penetrate the skin. Some people say that bilharzia isn't ever present in deep water, the centre of lakes, in cold or swift running water. It is certainly less likely to be here, as the snails like to live in the reeds or stagnant areas along the shore, but there is no guarantee. Luckily there is now a cure for bilharzia in tablet form, rather than the agonising series of injections

Bilharzia

that used to be involved, but it can be difficult to get rid of if not caught in time.

Water Water is safe to drink in all the main centres. If you are out in the bush, use a purifier. And if you are doing your own cooking, wash all fruit and vegetables you buy in a disinfectant solution as they are usually grown using natural fertilisers and untreated water.

The comfort of medical treatment varies greatly from government subsidised beds, which have thin mattresses and blankets, and often no sheets, to **Hospitals and** the private clinics which are easily equal to Western **doctors** hospitals. But whatever the conditions, the standard of medical care is good, only falling down in those cases that need sophisticated equipment which is not available in the country. General practitioners are all in private practice and do not come cheap, so adequate insurance is advised. There is a list of doctors in the front of each town's section of the phone book. The country is well covered by doctors, hospitals and clinics and you should never be more than a few hours away from medical attention, even if you are right out in the bush. As English is the official language, you won't have any difficulties explaining what is wrong.

National Parks
Zimbabwe is one of the most varied and beautiful of Africa's countries scenically, with every type of vegetation from the dry scrub of the Kalahari sands in the southwest to the rich cool forests and bracken-clad hills of the Eastern Highlands. And after devastation poaching, and disastrous development elsewhere in Africa, it is also one of the richest wildlife preserves left in the world.

A variety of There are 17 National Parks run by Government **preserves** National Parks of Zimbabwe, as well as numerous private game reserves. They range from game parks like the massive, internationally renowned Hwange in the northwest corner of the country to the tiny Ewanrigg botanical gardens near Harare. In total, some 11 percent of the country's area—

16

44,688 sq km—has been set aside as parkland. All the larger reserves have a variety of accommodation, which can be booked up to six months in advance. In the game parks you will only be allowed out of camp inside a vehicle unless on a guided walking tour with a qualified hunter. You will also only be allowed out of camp (or into the park, if you are staying outside) between 6am and 6pm, and will have to log in and out of the warden's office. This is a matter of security not only for the animals, but also for the visitors. If you haven't arrived back by 6, a search party will be sent out.

Outdoor rules   The following rules apply to all parks.

(1) Dogs are not allowed in any game area, rest camp, camping or caravan site.

(2) No children under the age of 14 are allowed to stay in the camps unless accompanied by an adult.

(3) You must not damage, injure, kill or remove any object, animal, vegetable or mineral within the park boundaries.

(4) All firearms must be declared to the warden on arrival.

(5) You are only allowed out of the car at designated points (most animals are exceptionally well camouflaged and you could be putting your life at risk by going for a walk).

(6) Be exceptionally careful not to start fires and report anyone you see being careless. (Bush fires are a major hazard, particularly in the dry season from July/August through to November, when the grass is tinder dry and fires sweep for miles before they can be checked. All too often it is something as simple as a broken bottle in the sun, or smoking ash from a cigarette that sparks the blaze.)

(7) No littering.

Park fees   At the larger parks—Chizarira, Kazuma Pan, Mana Pools, Matusadona and Hwange—there is an entry fee of Z$10 per adult and Z$4 per child for unlimited entry for seven days, or a once-only fee for day visitors of Z$4 per adult at Hwange.

At Zambezi, Chimanimani, Lake Robertson, Kyle, Mushandike, Matopos, Ngezi, McIlwaine, Sebakwe, Chinhoyi Caves, Ewanrigg and Vumba the fee for unlimited seven-day entry is Z$6 per adult, Z$2 per child, or one-day entry is Z$2 per adult and Z$1 per child. Fees should be paid at the park office on arrival.

Most of the parks are mentioned later in the book, but I have concentrated on those areas most commonly visited by tourists and the very remote are not. A full list and further information are available from and all bookings should be made through the Central Booking Office, National Parks of Zimbabwe, National Botanical Gardens, Sandringham Drive, PO Box 8151, Harare. Tel: Harare 706077. Telegrams: Parklife, Harare. Office hours: Monday to Friday, 7.45am—4.15pm.

Communications

Telephone and telex. The cost of a local call from a call box is 20c, for up to 3 minutes. The whole domestic phone network is crumbling, and it is often a matter of sheer luck as to whether you can get through, particularly in the rainy season, when even inter-city lines seem to come down with monotonous frequency after every storm. The problem is compounded by the shortage of lines which leads to overloading party-line systems. All long distance business is done by telex and you would do well to follow suit. In a real emergency, phone the UK (via satellite) and ask someone at home to phone for you. It's often the only way to get through. Don't use the phone for confidential conversations.

Post. Good and cheap. There are post offices in most towns, but it is far easier to buy your stamps in advance so that you can use post boxes. Airmail to Europe takes about five days. All post offices will sell stamps, register letters, offer telegrams and poste restante facilities.

Organisation

Get it right in Harare

Be prepared to spend your first two or three days in Harare, and do all your organisation before you leave the city. This not only includes booking accommodation, but car hire, sightseeing trips, transport, etc. Everything is done through a central office, and even if you are in Victoria Falls and want to hire a care from 100 metres down the road, you will have to wait while they try and get through to Harare to make the booking there. Resign yourself to this organising time, and you will save endless hassle in the end. Better still, try and get it all booked and paid for outside the country (as you are then let off the 15 percent sales tax). But still spend a day reconfirming everything. And be sure of what you want and stick to it—even the simplest change in your itinerary can cause many mutterings, furrowed brows and hours of confusion. The country is very well organised by African standards, but the system is just not geared up for high speed transactions.

Internal Transport

Air. Air Zimbabwe runs an excellent service with daily flights (or almost daily in some cases) to most of the main towns and tourist areas. The only area not served by air is the Eastern Highlands. Prices are cheap and as it is possible to hop on and off the plane at various stops along the way, you can travel halfway round the country for the equivalent of £100–£130. For instance, there is a flight from Harare to Victoria Falls which stops at Kariba and Hwange. From the Falls, you take a flight to Bulawayo, then return to Harare via Gweru. Distances are very long by road and some trips across the country will take a good day of hard driving. In addition, car hire is expensive, so it is often more economical to fly, as well as saving time if you're on a tight schedule.

Flying can be cheaper than driving

Air Zimbabwe runs a series of package tours called Flame Lily Tours based on their scheduled flights which include accommodation, food and some organised tours, although you are left to your own devices most of the time. These can be custom tailored to your own timetable. Book before you enter Zimbabwe if possible as you then won't have to pay the 15 percent sales tax.

Rail. The railway is another cheap alternative, and has recently become a tourist attraction in its own right, when Zimbabwe became the first country in the world to bring its steam locomotives out of storage. These are now used for most freight services and on some passenger trains. The rolling stock comes out of the ark, but is clean and reasonably comfortable. Almost all journeys are overnight and as they manage to string things out for an incredible time, you can get a good night's sleep.

Sleeping your way across the country

There are three classes: first, second and fourth! Fourth has overcrowded, wooden-slatted seats, but is very cheap (about Z$13 for the Harare-Mutare journey). Second class will give you a sleeper, with six to a compartment and costs about double, while First has four to a compartment and costs a bit more. You can buy bedding for an extra Z$10.45, and your bed will be made up for you. There is no food or drink on the trains (except between Bulawayo and Victoria Falls), so take your own supplies. There are kiosks at the main stations, but little variety.

For real enthusiasts, the best place to see the steam engines is in Bulawayo, where a permit available free from National Railways of Zimbabwe, Pancode Centre, Fife Street/10th Ave, Bulawayo, (tel: 363 523), gives you permission to photograph them, have a ride on the footplate, and visit the workshops and shunting yard. For those wishing to travel extensively by train, 'champagne' rail safaris have recently been introduced. Hauled by steam engines and using coaches from the Railway Museum, they last a week and run from Bulawayo to Hwange and Victoria Falls. Prices from £748. Contact Rail Safaris, Shop 4, Chancellor House Arcade (PO Box 4070), Harare. Tel: 736056. Telex: 22068.

Road. With a few minor exceptions, driving is easy. About the only beneficial effect of the war was the building-up of an excellent road network, partly to help with troop movements, and partly because it was far more difficult to mine a tarred road.

Easy driving The towns are now all connected by well-designed and maintained roads. They stretch into the distance with scarcely a bend, and driving is fast. The only real danger is of hitting a stray cow or antelope, a particular hazard at night. Even most of the side roads are tarred, although some of the least used will be single strip with a wide dirt bank either side for passing. As far as I know, none of the old strip roads (two parallel strips of tar, the width of your wheels) are still in use. Right off the beaten track, and in the game parks, the roads are gravel or dirt, and these may be more difficult in the rainy season, but there is nowhere you could not manage in an ordinary saloon car.

The roads in the towns are very wide, often as wide as a six-lane motorway. These date back to the first settlements of the earliest pioneers who had to make sure they had space to turn a wagon and a span of 16 oxen. Now they make sure that the worst traffic jam lasts five minutes and there is always room to park.

Zimbabwe, as an ex-British colony, drives on the left. Road signs are familiar, with a few additions such as elephant or lion crossing warnings! The country is completely metricated and all distances, speeds, etc, are in kilometres. The official maximum speed limit on open roads is 100 km per hour.

Fuel. Petrol and diesel are both freely available. Petrol is cheap, (Z$2.58 a litre at the time of writing) but is not good quality, often being mixed with ethanol. Diesel is cheaper still. There are garages or pumps in all the towns, some villages and even at some of the more isolated hotels, so it is rare to be too far away from supplies. However, once in the game parks or right away from the main roads you

For cars . . .

could have problems and should carry a jerry can with you.

and for stoves You may have some problems getting hold of cooking fuels such as camping gas. There is gas for sale, but for the large, heavy, refillable canisters rather than the lightweight throw-away kind most travellers are used to. Paraffin is still used as a primary cooking fuel, however, and is easy to come by. I would recommend taking a stove that will work on a variety of fuels, eg paraffin, solid fuel and petrol.

Car Hire. The three large international car hire companies—Avis, Hertz and Europcar—all have bases in Zimbabwe and operate offices in all main centres. Their cars are new and usually in good condition, as they work to the normal ruling of a rental life of 18 months to two years. Because of the desperate shortage of foreign currency and the resultant difficulty in bringing in new cars, however, they are also expensive—from Z$120 per day plus 90c to Z$1.65 per kilometre. Even if you want to have a car, use public transport on long routes and hire separately in each town.

Money-saving strategy

There are also a few small local firms, but these are just as expensive and generally far less reliable. They haven't got the international backing to help them bring in new vehicles and while Zimbabweans are extraordinarily adept at keeping ancient vehicles on the road, there are no spare parts and most repairs are carried out with a lot of ingenuity and a ball of string.

Taxis. There are plenty of taxis in the main towns—Harare, Bulawayo, Gweru and Mutare; usually geriatric Renault 4s with little space inside. They are all run by private companies, and while they are all metered, the charge per kilometre is not yet set by the government (although they are talking of altering this) and can vary quite considerably. I took the same trip across Harare several times using a different firm each time and the cost varied from Z$1.70 to Z$3.25. The standard should be

Local buses in Harare

around \$2 a kilometer with a \$1 start-up charge. The three largest and most reliable firms are Rixi, Creamline and A1, so look for these first.

There is also a problem with copy-cats—small, unrelated companies, or even single drivers who paint their cars in similar colours to or use a logo virtually indistinguishable from those of the more reliable firms. These set their meters at a far higher rate. I never encountered anyone who tried to turn the meter off and name their own price.

Taxis get more expensive outside Harare and Bulawayo. Nearly double in Mutare, and in Kariba the one and only taxi can charge what it likes—and does. Some friends of mine were charged over Z\$50 for a journey of about 6 or 7 km.

Airport buses. There are buses from all the airports into the nearest town centre. In Harare, Bulawayo and Victoria Falls they are run by Air Zimbabwe. In Harare they go every hour (or half-hour at certain times of day) from the Air Zimbabwe headquarters building opposite Meikles Hotel. Tickets (Z\$20 one way) are sold as you board, and I have never had any difficulty getting a seat. Elsewhere, there are only a couple of flights a day at the most, and a bus run by a local tour company will deliver outgoing passengers and pick up the incoming ones. It is probably sensible to book before you leave Harare, but you shouldn't have any problems if you go to the UTC/Buffalo Safaris desk on arrival As private companies, they will charge more. At Kariba, it cost me Z$80 each way to get to my hotel.

Inter-city buses. Perhaps a generous title for buses that would have been retired with full honours at least ten years ago in Europe or the United States. However, they continue to work, chugging up and down the roads with great reliability and only a little smoke, providing the best and fastest means of long distance travel in the country. Express Motorways is the largest operator, running regular trips between all the main towns. The price is about the same as First Class on the train, but the journey takes about half the time. They are perfectly comfortable and longer journeys include a loo and coffee stop of about half an hour.

Faster than trains

Local buses. There are plenty of local buses, which are very cheap and will get you into the areas off the main roads, but these have several disadvantages. Firstly, they are always bulging at the seams and you are very likely to find yourself sitting on a pile of cases, a couple of children and a goat. Secondly, they are very erratic, and unless you are starting from the main depot in the centre of town, you could wander helplessly for days at a time, trying to find a bus and get it to stop for you. A large number of totally separate companies are involved and none seems to publish a timetable. I asked ten different people about one route and got ten different answers. When I pointed this out, ten pairs of hands were raised skywards in a charming gesture of helplessness. I gave up.

Hitchhiking. Hitching is in the main safe, although the general rule about not hitching on your own also applies here. Start early enough to make sure you reach your destination before dark, as predators, both animal and human, make it unsafe to be stranded in the bush overnight.

Sharing costs   People are generally friendly and helpful and you shouldn't have too much difficulty getting a lift on reasonably busy roads. Some people may suggest that you share costs, so don't automatically expect to get there completely free. They will never ask for unreasonable amounts.

Accommodation

The chief problem with accommodation in Zimbabwe is that there is very little in the way of good, cheap accommodation equivalent to the bed and breakfast or pension. There are plenty of good hotels, and excellent self-catering chalets and camp sites, but not much alternative for someone on a limited budget who doesn't want the hassles of cooking, but wants a little respectability. Two-tier pricing for foreigners was brought in by law a few years ago at all the top hotels (including all those run by Zimbabwe Sun, although, interestingly, not at those run by the Zimbabwe Tourism Development Corporation). This means that while the lower end of the market is still cheap by British standards, top hotel prices are now on a par with Western ones. A room that a Zimbabwean citizen would get for Z$100 could well cost a foreigner US$100. If you want the luxury that always used to be associated with travel in Zimbabwe, it is now an expensive place to visit.

Superb service   **Hotels.** If one thing categorises accommodation in Zimbabwe, it is superb service. Even the smaller good hotels run 24-hour room service, shoe-cleaning, same-day laundry, etc. (One hotel manager explained that it is so difficult to get hold of electrical gadgets such as kettles, it is easier and cheaper to run full room service than to provide tea-making facilities in the rooms.) Stay more than one night and you will find yourself treated like royalty in the morning as everyone from the cleaners to the head waiter greets you by name and asks tenderly after your night's rest. It is all too easy to sink into the luxury of the lifestyle and never want to struggle out again.

There are only three five-star hotels in the country, all in Harare—the Sheraton, a massive gold tower, likened by one resident to a cigar box; Meikles, the first hotel to be opened in the country, but now a forbidding 1960s concrete block; and the Monomotapa. There are also several four star hotels in Harare, Victoria Falls and the Eastern Highlands. In most of them, the architecture and furnishings are a little tired, and the food is of a poor quality in comparison to their European and American equivalents, but they are comfortable, efficient **Palace of** and friendly. The best is probably the Victoria Falls **delight** Hotel, one of the oldest buildings in the country, a palace of Italianate colonial architecture that is a delight to look at and a luxury to stay in.

The majority of decent hotels in Zimbabwe fall into the three-star bracket. It is one of the quirks in the system that while nothing in the country will match up to the great five-star hotels of the world, the medium range is far, far better than the European equivalent, providing a level of real lux-**Tropical** ury to the foreign visitor. The best of these is the **country house** Troutbeck Inn at Nyanga, the closest one can get **hotel** in the tropics to an English country house hotel, with roaring log fires, chintzy sofas and a view of mountains, lakes and pines.

There are some good one- or two-star hotels in Harare, while in some of the small towns such as Rusape, Chipinge, etc, that are off the tourist beat there will only be one or, at a pinch, two hotels/motels, which serve as the local pub and disco as well as providing accommodation. These small town hotels are all similar, a long, low building with a verandah along the street front, and probably a corrugated iron roof. These are still quite adequate, but not wildly cheap in comparison to those slightly higher up the scale.

Rooms by the hour

Of course, there are also some very cheap, unstarred hotels, but these are often the type of places that rent by the hour and you could find yourself subjected to unexpected entertainment in the wee small hours. Ask for local recommendations before making your booking.

Self-catering. Self-catering accommodation is very well represented in a country where outdoor life is one of its greatest appeals and the weather is almost always good enough for camping. Campsites in most places tend to be small and charming, although some of the main city sites are a little impersonal. They provide toilets and washing facilities with plenty of hot water (often heated by a wood stove at the back in the more remote areas without electricity), will usually have laundry facilities, braai (barbecue) areas and will often provide wood. There is also normally a caretaker who will sometimes do odd jobs for you if required. Camping costs about Z$6–16 a night.

Campsites

Cottages and rondaavels

Many campsites are shared by groups of self-catering cottages, chalets or rondaavels (large and more luxurious versions of the round, mud-walled native huts). These too come with the basics, and probably a cleaner to come in, make the beds, chop the vegetables, stack new wood, etc. You will have to provide all your own food, as well as salt and pepper, bedding, cutlery, and in some areas your own drinking water as well. A rondaavel will cost from about Z$30 a night. Out of town, self-catering may well be the most satisfactory way to live, as you are further away from civilisation, with room for walking, and with the wildlife on your doorstep—often literally. There is little that is more evocative of Africa than sitting under the stars listening to the crickets and the frogs, nostrils filled with the hot, sweet smell of the bush, overlaid by the gentle hiss of a paraffin lamp and the occasional high-pitched buzz as another mosquito swoops in to attack.

It is possible to camp on private land if you are

given permission, but it is inadvisable to pitch camp by the wayside. You may fall foul of the law if you do so, and there is a danger from bandits. You will rarely find any campsite so overcrowded that it becomes unpleasant, and they are easily affordable. It is sensible to book first if you are planning to go during the height of the season (April/May, August/September and over Christmas) as the chalets and many campsites, particularly in the National Parks, book up many months in advance.

Food

The food is generally unexciting, but edible. There are few specialities and in the main the middle class, black and white, eats English-style meat and two veg, or variations on that theme.

Local stodge
The local staple of rural Africans is a type of stiff porridge called sadza. This is made from mealies (sweetcorn), ground into flour and mixed with water. Most of the water is then wrung out until it forms a stiff dough which is dipped into meat and gravy (nyama). Sadza serves much the same purpose that Yorkshire pudding used to do in the 19th C (although it is certainly more nutritious) by filling people up with stodge. Nyama can be any sort of meat and is usually unspecified—anything from game or beef to the more usual goat or elderly mutton. The dish should be tried as it is such an integral part of the culture, but be warned, the quality varies dramatically and it can be truly revolting.

Meat dishes
Meat is the staple further up the social scale—particularly steak, which is ubiquitous, and dirt cheap by European standards. It would be easy to eat steak three times a day if you so desired—and some people do. It is often the only 'safe' item on the menu in a country where chefs are taught to take perfectly good ingredients and mangle them.

It is unlikely that you will go to Zimbabwe and not attend at least one braaivleis (barbecue). The braai is an integral part of the social scene and an integral part of the braai is boerevoes, a hard, spicy sausage, Afrikaans in origin and quite delicious.

The other common meat dish (or snack) to be tried is biltong—salted meat cut into strips and sun-dried. Originally designed to preserve meat in the hot climate before the days of refrigeration, it can be reconstituted by soaking, but these days is more often eaten as it comes for a snack. They say that **Ostrich and** the best—the haute cuisine of biltong—is ostrich, **elephant...** but it can be made of anything from elephant down to the humble cow.

Many of the better restaurants will have at least one game option on the menu. A real speciality, which I couldn't bring myself to try, is crocodiles' **crocodile...** tails. I thought the whole idea was a hoax until a visit to a crocodile farm persuaded me of the truth. Crocodiles are farmed for their skins, so the tail meat is a lucrative by-product. The rest of the croco-dile is fed back to its friends! At the Hwange Safari **impala and** Lodge during my last visit, both impala and **warthog** warthog were also on the menu. I had impala, which tasted rather like braising steak. Friends who had the warthog said, as might be expected, that it was a more pungent pork.

If you are on a budget and eating out, eat in the middle of the day as most of the large hotels run buffets that are amazing value. A vast range of salads, one hot dish and a selection of puddings— **Best value** as much as you can eat for a set price. The best **meals** value I discovered was the Pool Deck at the Mono-motapa in Harare where I paid Z$20. The most expensive was the Victoria Falls Hotel, where it was Z$35. Many places also have a set menu in the evening, which can also be good value, although more expensive. The most I paid for any meal—for five courses and coffee—was Z$45. And the meal, at Troutbeck, a hotel renowned throughout the coun-try, was excellent by any standards.

Consider eating at the hotels even if you are not staying there. The hotel bars double as pubs (there **Socialising** are no English style pubs in the country) and social life revolves around them. You can easily pay more for an inferior meal in a restaurant, though in Harare there is a wider choice, especially if you have transport and are prepared to venture beyond the centre of the city for a meal. Outside the four main towns you won't have much of an option.

Drink

Everything comes long and cold, usually with ice. Zimbabweans consider the British longing for warm bitter and Scotch without the rocks as strange in the extreme. But after a few days in the tropical heat you will begin to see their reasoning. If you are not converted, remember to specify exactly how you want your drink served.

Beer   All clear beer is lager. It comes in half-litre bottles and two brands, Lion and Castle, of which Lion is the stronger. It costs around Z$2 a bottle. The only other beer is the local brew, called Chibuku, which is a cloudy white and made (mostly) from sorghum. It is very cheap way to get drunk, but is only sold in the beer halls and waiters will be shocked and extremely stuffy if you ask for it in a better establishment. If you do want to try it, it is served in plastic buckets that hold a quart—the idea (but rarely the practice) being that it should be shared by the group. Visit a beer hall even if you don't want to try it. They are noisy, crowded and great fun.

Spirits   Variations on all spirits are available but expensive. They are clearly divided into local, which tend to be cane spirit with flavouring and therefore rough, or imported, which are all the normal brands, but very expensive (Z$10 a tot in some cases). The exception is the local gin, which is good and cheap. Liqueurs also have their local counterparts and some (such as Triple Sec, the orange liqueur) are quite drinkable. If you are going to drink local whisky or brandy, drown it (another good reason for taking your drinks long). Tots are the equivalent of an English double.

Wine   Zimbabwe is a wine producing country, and you won't find anything on sale except the local produce. I've had a couple of disasters but Zimbabwe is now producing several wines which, while they couldn't compete internationally, are quite drinkable and won't leave you at death's door. The cheapest will be about Z$12 a bottle.

Non-alcoholic drinks

Non-alcoholic, very cheap and a drink perfectly adapted for the climate is the rock shandy, probably one of the commonest drinks in Zimbabwe and completely unknown elsewhere. A few drops of Angostura Bitters, a long glass half filled with lemonade, and topped up with soda water, finished with some ice and a slice of lemon. An alternative is the slightly sweeter Malawi shandy which replaces the lemonade with ginger beer.

Tipping

Zimbabwe is still a remarkably polite country and unlike many places a tip is still treated as a bonus and not a right. The service will still be impeccable and come with a smile if you don't pay extra for the privilege. I didn't find a single restaurant where an automatic service charge had been added on. Ten percent is considered generous most of the time. I found myself converting the amount for a while and feeling embarassed by how little it came to in sterling, but salaries and cost of living are also lower.

Politeness and impeccable service

Porters, who abound at all stations, airports, hotels, etc, should be given 20–30c per bag. This can actually prove expensive as there seems to be a general alarm if you have to carry your bag from one side of the foyer to the other yourself. Some hotels run a staff box at the cashier's counter, so you can pay once at the end of your stay.

There are some beggars in the towns, but they will generally sit quietly huddled in a doorway, a tin bowl in front of them, and will not harrass or proposition you.

Entertainment

Western cultural events

If you are looking for flights of Western culture, this is the wrong place to come. The country is not totally bereft. Amateur theatre groups exist in almost all the towns, and are usually terribly keen, but except for Reps Theatre in Harare, plays are spaced fairly widely and are only on for two or three nights. The same is true for concerts. Occasionally a foreign group will tour (the Bolshoi Ballet can rarely have performed in more unusual settings), but they are very infrequent.

African music　The greatest treat in the country is the native African music, a raw, repetitive chant that weaves everchanging patterns around a basic, simple theme. The sense of tune and rhythm both seem completely natural—one person starts singing and everyone around spontaneously breaks into six part harmony. It brings a lump to the throat and tears of inadequacy to the Western eye. Zimbabwean pop music has recently become known across the world, with groups such as the Bundu Boys and Thomas Mapfumo creating a renaissance of interest in African Music. They use traditional themes and instruments and spice then up with electronics to create a sound that is both unique and totally wonderful. When not touring, both groups and a number of others play regularly at nightclubs in Harare, Mbare and Highfields. Check local press for details.

Sport　Sport is the most popular pastime—cricket, tennis, golf and football, which is rapidly taking over from rugby as the national sport. And, of course, swimming. You will never stay anywhere (unless you take off into the bush) that doesn't have access to a swimming pool. Most hotels and many homes have their own, and the day—and often the evening—is spent around it.

Zimbabwe is a place that believes in socialising. Dinner parties, parties, dances and braais (barbecues) are all an important part of life. Clubs also play a greater role than we are used to, not only the sports clubs, but such institutions as Round Table, Rotary and Lions. And each of the main towns has a gentleman's club, run along traditional lines, with magnificent dining facilities, and one

Clubs

room into which women are allowed to slink apologetically and with as little disturbance as possible. There are reciprocal arrangements with many British clubs.

It is incredibly easy to meet people and the conversation will often result in an invitation to a meal, if not to stay. People will take you at face value and open their homes to you in a fashion long since **The importance** vanished in most Western societies. For many of **of socialising** them, you provide a good opportunity to find out what is happening in the outside world and you will be cross-questioned about fashion, music, and other day to day aspects of life.

Nightspots There are one or two decent nightclubs in Harare and Bulawayo for those with a taste for the more sophisticated, and there are casinos at Kariba, Victoria Falls and Nyanga.

Opening Hours

Shops: 8am to 5pm Monday to Friday; 8am to 12 noon Saturday. Most shut for lunch between 1 and 2 and Wednesday is a half-day, except in the large shops in main towns.

Banks: 8.30am to 2pm Monday, Tuesday, Thursday, Friday; 8.30am to 12 noon Wednesday; 8.30am to 11am Saturday.

Post Offices: 8.30am to 4pm Monday to Friday; 8.30am to 11.30am Saturday. The public telex office in Harare is open 8.30am to 5pm Monday to Friday; 8.30am to 11.30am Saturday.

Liquor licensing hours (opening times):
Hotels: 10.30am to 11.30pm Monday to Saturday; 10.30am to 10.30pm Sunday.
Restaurants: 11am to 3pm and 4pm to 11.30pm every day.
Bars: 10.30am to 11pm every day.
Nightclubs: 8pm to 3am Monday to Saturday.
Bottle stores: 8am to 8pm every day.
Petrol stations: 6am to 6pm every day.

Electricity

220V AC; three square-pin plugs. Usually reliable, but take a flashlight, as there are often brief power cuts outside the main centres.

Weights and Measures

Zimbabwe employs the metric system.

Temperature

Fahrenheit	=	Celsius
122		50
113		45
110		43.3
107.6		42
104		40
102.2		39
100		37.8
98.6		37
96.8		36
95		35
93.2		34
91.4		33
90		32
87.8		31
86		30
84.2		29
80		26.7
75		23.9
70		21
65		18.3
60		15.6
55		12.8
50		10
45		7.2
40		4
32		0
23		−5
14		−10
0		−17.8

Fahrenheit into Celsius: subtract 32 from Fahrenheit temperature, then multiply by 5, then divide by 9.
Celsius into Fahrenheit: multiply Celcius by 9, then divide by 5, then add 32.

Linear Measure

0.39 inches	1 centimetre
1 inch	2.54 centimetres
1 foot (12 in)	0.30 metres
1 yard (3 ft)	0.91 metres
39.37 inches	1 metre
0.62 miles	1 kilometre
1 mile (5280 ft)	1.61 kilometres
3 miles	4.8 kilometres
10 miles	16 kilometres
60 miles	98.6 kilometres
100 miles	160.9 kilometres

Square Measure

1 sq foot	0.09 sq metres
1 sq yard	0.84 sq metres
1.20 sq yards	1 sq metre
1 acre	0.405 hectares
1 sq mile	259 hectares or 2.59 sq km

Weight

0.04 ounces	1 gram
1 ounce	28.35 grams
1 pound	453.59 grams
2.20 pounds	1 kilogram
1 ton (2000 lbs)	907.18 kilograms
	1 metric tonne = 1000 kilograms

Liquid Measure

0.22 imperial gallons	1 litre
0.26 US gallons	1 litre
1 US gallon	3.79 litres
1 imperial gallon	4.55 litres

Public Holidays

1 January: New Year's Day.
Good Friday, Easter Saturday and Monday.
18 April: Independence Day.
1 May: Workers' Day.
25 and 26 May: Africa Day.
11 and 12 August: Heroes' Day.
25 and 26 December: Christmas Day and Boxing Day.

Time

Local time is GMT +2. When it is noon GMT, it is 2pm in Zimbabwe.

Shopping and What to Take with You

The shops look very empty if you are coming in from Europe, but there are few essentials that you can't buy. There just isn't the choice. A basic rule of thumb is that anything imported is vastly more expensive, so buy the local version instead. Years of sanctions meant that industry became extremely resourceful and there is a local substitute for most things.

Imports are very expensive

Food is cheap in comparison to Europe; staples are about a third of the price. Fruit and vegetables are generally not lush, but they are good and plentiful. You will find it difficult to get an apple worth eating (there are a few places that grow them in the Eastern Highlands, and the Clairmont estate runs an excellent fruit stall in the Nyanga Mountains) but tropical fruits such as watermelons, pineapples, mangoes, guavas and pawpaws are wonderful and incredibly cheap from roadside stalls.

Basic cotton clothing is easy to find and good quality, but you should take anything more glamorous with you. Likewise shoes. There are some local prints, caftans, etc on sale, but in the main these seem to have died along with the ethnic spasm of the seventies.

Medicines . . .

Take a comprehensive medical chest with you. You can buy basics, but they are not cheap, and should you require any more specialist medication, it is not certain you will be able to get it.

films . . .   Film is obtainable in the main centres these days, but you should always check the date on the box to make sure it is not old stock. You will be unlikely to find much of anything outside the cities. Film will cost you Z$30 a roll without processing, which can cost another Z$40–50. Video tapes are more difficult to find, especially the mini-cassettes for camcorders, so take plenty with you.

Likewise take batteries, which are available, but are poor quality and will only last a couple of hours, and tapes, which cost a fortune to buy there. Basically anything electrical is worth rather more than gold dust (which is available locally). Prices are about three times what you would pay new abroad. If you want to take small thank-you presents, cheap calculators, digital watches, hairdriers, etc, are ideal.

Souvenirs

There is a wide range of souvenirs on sale, catering for all tastes and every purse. Some are tacky, such as the glass paperweights with a lump of 'genuine elephant bullshit' in them that I saw in a Harare gift shop, and many are clichés, such as a tremendous selection of topees made in anything from elephant hide to cotton for all the would-be Zambezi explorers, but most are based on the local crafts of basketry, pottery and beadwork, wood and stone carving.

Basketry   Especially in the south of the country, there are basket markets beside the roads out in the bush. Stop and walk around. Prices are low to start with and some judicious haggling will bring them down even further. Apart from useful containers for putting things in, the range will include every conceivable shape of hat to basketry baboons.

Crochet   In the Kariba area, the local women have taken to crochet in a big way and the sides of the roads are covered with a spider's web of white lace tablecloths and place mats. The material is generally a fairly coarse cotton, but the work and design are

Hand-made crochet lace tablecloths and bedspreads

excellent, and at Z$30–50 for a large tablecloth they are ridiculously cheap, especially considering the vast amount of time and effort that has gone into producing them.

Handmade pottery

Most of the pottery in the souvenir shops is hand-made, unglazed, and often fire-baked in the traditional manner, which means that it is beautiful to look at, has a wonderful sooty smell, and isn't terribly good at holding water. It is also rather heavy and fragile to be transported easily. There is one commercial pottery which uses local design to produce beautiful, very useable stoneware. This is the Mzilikaze Arts Co-operative in Bulawayo.

Attractive stones

One of Zimbabwe's main sources of wealth is its rich and varied mineral deposits that have not only turned mining into a major industry, but also produce a fabulous range of stones, precious, semi-precious and just pretty. The most famous are probably the Sandawana emeralds, mined just outside Bulawayo. Their quality is generally not high— they tend to be pale in colour and flawed—but they are nevertheless a good buy. There are numerous semi-precious stones such as tiger-eye and rose quartz which you can literally pick up lying around on the ground in the right areas and are incredibly cheap to buy, either as polished eggs, or as gem-stone jewellery. Others, such as malachite, are more expensive, but still far cheaper than in Europe.

Everywhere you go you are guaranteed to find street vendors with a row of hippos and rhinos in front of them, of all shapes, sizes and colours. Some are of local hardwoods, such as mukwa, **Carved animals** mahogany or ebony, but most will be of soapstone, which is found in an amazing variety of different colours within Zimbabwe. It is very soft and easy to carve and is therefore the most popular of all the stones to work for mass tourist consumption. Most of the animals will be identical, but occasionally you can find something of more interest.

In the grounds of the Victoria Falls Hotel there is a souvenir shop that specialises in traditional dance masks. Some are massive, a metre or more in length and hung with fearsome fringes— **Dance masks** wonderful if you have a huge house, and a private plane to take them home, but totally overpowering otherwise—which will cost upwards of Z$200, but they scale down from these to miniature, for every pocket. They are all carved by the dancers who give displays in the arena next door each evening, so if you ask they will tell you the history of the particular mask that interests you as well as its tribal symbolism. You will also find drums everywhere you go, at any size, and varying from the plain to the ornately carved.

One thing to watch out for when buying wooden objects is that you always buy a hard wood. Some of the soft woods are extremely susceptible to infestation by various pests, and are therefore not welcomed by customs authorities back home.

At the expensive end of the souvenir range comes carved ivory. Zimbabwe's elephant herds are the **Ivory** most successful left in the world, to the extent that major cull is needed every few years to stop them stripping the land of all vegetation. As a result, there is still plenty of ivory for sale. If you buy any, remember that there is now a total, worldwide ban on ivory trading and it will certainly be confiscated by customs if found. There is also a wide variety of elephant hide products.

Shona sculpture   In the last 20 years there has been an explosion of artistic talent amongst black Zimbabweans, helped by a few far-sighted people who founded artists' cooperatives. Apart from traditional wood carving, the Shona had no history of sculpting, and the magnificent art that is now being produced has little resemblance to traditional design, being more akin in style to the smooth, squat, abstract figures of the Eskimos. Worked in highly polished hard stone, from verdite to granite, the Shona sculptures sell from Z$500 to Z$5000, for work which would cost several times as much in Europe. It can't be too long before these artists are 'discovered' by the art world, but meantime their work is an amazing bargain. Galleries will ship if you don't want to lug 50 kilos of stone home yourself.

Photography

No permits are needed and there are no restrictions on photography, although you could find yourself having a long session down at the local police station if you photograph anything even vaguely connected with the military. On the Kopje in Harare, for instance, there are several notices warning you not to take photos, which seem more and more mysterious as there is nothing to see, let alone anything to tempt you to waste a film—until you round a corner and see one small gun emplacement and three soldiers drinking tea. After all the fuss, it took a great deal of willpower not to photograph them. The view from the top, it should be said, is wonderful, and well worth some film.

Light conditions   The light is very strong and the colours, particularly in summer, are vivid, great sweeps of scarlet bougainvillea and rich gold savannah. It is perfectly suited to Kodachrome, although the midday light in summer is often too harsh for good photography, the sky turning white and bleaching the landscape. A warming filter would be useful in these conditions. Summer storms can provide striking photos, but mid-winter is frustrating, with sullen skies and the land parched to a nearly even brown. Sunrises and sunsets are usually magnificent.

Photographing people . . .
People usually don't mind being photographed if you ask first. I have never been asked for money, except by the witch doctors/fortune tellers at Victoria Falls, who are there purely for the tourists. You will, however, find it very difficult to get natural poses as everyone will all straighten up, flash their widest grins and wait politely. Several people walked up to me in the street and asked if I would take their picture. I pointed out that I could neither pay them nor give them a Polaroid print but they said that didn't matter. They just enjoyed it. On one occasion, by the time I had taken the shot, I had a queue of seven other people standing behind me asking to be next.

and wildlife
There are plenty of opportunities for wildlife photography, so take a telephoto lens.

Crime

On the whole, Zimbabwe is an honest country. Travelling as a woman alone I never felt frightened. The people are generally very kind and friendly and an appeal for assistance is unlikely to be taken as an excuse to rip you off. Neither will you have to count your change too carefully or guard against the numerous sleight of hand tricks encountered in some Third World countries. Errors are likely to be just that. Long may it last.

An honest people
There is crime, of course, and sadly it is on the increase. With a desperate shortage of vehicles and spare parts, there has been a rapid increase in the number of thefts of or from vehicles, with professional gangs, capable of stripping a vehicle down to a bare metal hulk in a couple of minutes, working the cities. So lock up securely and try not to leave

vehicles unguarded. There is also more violent crime, including muggings and rape, than there was formerly. In general, however, the streets are pretty safe to walk around, even at night as long as you are reasonably sensible.

A recent surge in official corruption, stretching from the highest to the lowest, has made it tragically common for a bribe to be requested. It is not always necessary to comply, so do say no unless it is the very last resort.

Security

A high level of safety and stability

Until a few years ago, Zimbabwe laboured under years of bad press during the war and immediately after independence. In fact Zimbabwe is now safer and more stable than virtually anywhere else in Africa. The government is extremely keen that nothing should mar the rebirth of the tourist industry and has been careful not to place tourists in jeopardy. There is free access anywhere in the country. Nevertheless, it is as well to be cautious in some areas.

There are still a few bandits in some remote parts, for the most part one-time freedom fighters who kept their weapons and turned renegade on independence. And in the far northwest and southeast of the country there have been a few nasty encounters with poachers who, having shot out the game further to the north, have turned their attentions to Zimbabwe's elephants and rhinos, operating with helicopters and machine guns. Zimbabwe operates a shoot-to-kill policy against poachers, so they are extremely dangerous, but it is rare that the average traveller, however intrepid, will be far enough off the beaten track to encounter them.

Trouble spots

Matabeleland, in the southwest of the country, around Bulawayo, is now safe, with all outward political and tribal differences solved, although there is still a great deal of muttering on both sides. Check with locals before heading into the wilder areas of the Eastern Highlands which border on

The South African connection

Mozambique. There is technically a ceasefire in Mozambique but MNR rebels do make occasional raids across the border often sacking and massacring whole villages. The risk is remote, but should not be ignored.

Officialdom is still extremely wary of South Africa, which means that any hint of white militarism is likely to be regarded as provocation. Steps will be taken accordingly, and while you are unlikely to be jailed, you may have to spend a few awkward hours answering questions.

WILDLIFE BACKGROUND

Dawn is just breaking, but already the earth has that warm, sweet, sooty smell and already the doves are cooing in the trees outside. The last thing you heard as you went to sleep was the high pitched sawing of the Christmas beetle or perhaps the almost human wail of a bushbaby. There is little more evocative of Africa than its sounds and smells.

Most people assume that you need to visit the game parks to see Africa's wildlife. In fact, while they are certainly the best places to see big game, **Indoor** you can see plenty just by looking along the road-**wildlife . . .** side—or even at your bedroom wall. You will probably only just be opening your eyes when you hear a scratching noise above you and a gecko careers past in hot pursuit of a spider. Most homes have their complement of wildlife. The spiders eat the mosquitoes, the geckos the spiders, and the geckos can be caught and moved if they get so large they are disturbing you—unless the cat has eaten them first.

Go into the garden and there is a feast of delights. Locusts (a delicacy) go lumbering past, whirring **and garden** their wings; a chameleon rocks slowly on a twig, **beasties** silently stalking a stick insect; a chongalolo (the local millipedes which can grow up to 30 cm long) curls defensively into a tight ball as your foot blocks its path; a blue-headed agama streaks up the side of the house and a small flock of yellow wax bills has landed on the lawn to mop up the unwary crickets and grasshoppers.

The garden is a riot of colour—bougainvillea, jasmine, honeysuckle and golden shower cascading down the garage walls, pointsettias the size of trees nestle beside the firs, while behind them grow bananas, lemons and avocados. Hibiscus, geranium, dahlia, lily. Almost everything grows here.

Cautiously into Walk along a narrow path into the bush and you **the bush** will see the marks of curious antelope or leopard that came close in the night, or meet a tortoise lumbering out in search of worms. As the day warms up, take care of where you put your feet, just in case you step on a sunbathing puff adder stretched across the path.

It is very rare for anyone to run into problems with the wildlife in Zimbabwe, but however beautiful, remember that it is truly wild and treat it with respect. Mammals may be carrying rabies and anything could give you tetanus.

On the other hand it is all too easy to be unduly frightened by the new and strange. I have kept dinner parties shuddering for hours with stories of the boomslang that our kitten caught, or the cobras that lived in the garden, or the time when my white mice were eaten by a black mamba. It would be easy to make someone believe that you couldn't stir outside the house without fighting for your life three times before breakfast. But these were stories built up over 14 years. You will, in all probablity, never see a snake or any of the other nasties around.

Things to Beware of
Spiders. There are three main types that will give you a very nasty bite: the baboon spider, huge, pink and hairy; the hunting spider, equally huge and hairy, but black; and the button spider which is very small and black. The common house spider is large and black but flat and is of no danger to anything but mosquitoes. They are a Good Thing to have in your bedroom. There are many other varieties as well, some of which are poisonous.

Flying insects.
Malaria risk

Mosquitoes: These can be malarial and are always unpleasant. Use a repellant in the summer evenings and at night, and wear clothes that cover arms and ankles at dusk.

Hornets: These are not actually hornets at all but a rather large and ferocious wasp. They are easily recognisable by their very long, thin, orange and black stripy body and two long stings trailing behind. They nest under the eaves or even inside the house.

Bees: There are several different bees of varying degrees of ferocity. On the whole African bees are bad-tempered creatures that will attack anything they don't like. And they don't like a variety of smells, including perfume, onions, garlic, alcohol and cheese, and they don't like being disturbed. They are also attracted to the smell of panic, so if you find yourself near a swarm, try your damnedest to keep calm.

Flies: There are many different flies in the country, most of which are irritating, especially in the bush, when they are attracted by sweat. But the only one that can be dangerous is the tsetse fly, which is now thankfully very rare in Zimbabwe. This is up **Sleeping sickness** to a centimetre long and has a sharp, painful bite, but more seriously carries sleeping sickness. It has been eradicted in almost all farming areas and you are only likely to find them now when way off the beaten track. They hang around in shaded areas near water.

Others: None of the other flying insects are either dangerous or unpleasant, but they can be alarming. The air at night round any lamp will be thick with some of the 500-odd species of moth to be found in the country, many of which are huge clumsy beasts with hairy bodies that are quite likely to sideswipe you in passing. The yellow and black Emperor dragonfly which is the largest in the country can reach a wingspan of 13 cm and can do speeds of up to 50 kph. Grasshoppers can be 5 cm long and stick insects have been recorded at 30 cm.

Snakes. There are 75 species of snake known to live in Zimbabwe of which about a third are harmless. Of the rest there are few which can do real damage to an animal as large as a human, and these are listed below.

Snakes tend to have very poor eyesight and

instead rely on a keen sense of smell and vibration. If they hear you coming they will usually vanish, though a few, such as the puff adder, rely on camouflage instead and will just lie quietly. The most likely places to meet snakes are on paths or rocks where they come out to sun themselves or, if they are shade lovers, under those same rocks or in hollow logs, but there are also a few tree dwellers. If you are going off the beaten track, wear stout boots and trousers as most bites are on the ankles and these may shield you. If you are worried about snakes in your bed, put Jeyes' Fluid round the house or tent. They hate the smell and will not come near it.

Keeping snakes out of your bed

If someone in your party is bitten, keep everything as calm as possible. They will probably go into shock and panic will further increase the heart beat, and speed up the poison's progress through the body. Cutting the wound and sucking out the poison is a waste of time and could actually be harmful, and tourniquets are only useful for a limited time in certain cases. Always treat for shock, immobilise the limb, and get to a hospital or clinic as soon as possible. Be prepared if necessary to give artificial respiration on the way.

Treatment for snakebite

There are two types of serum on sale, a general one which works on most adders, vipers and cobras, and one specifically for mambas. If you feel you will be in a high-risk situation take these with you and have a lesson in their use from a qualified medical practitioner before you go. But most importantly always get medical help as soon as possible, and always treat the bite as hostile. If possible, kill the snake and take it to the hospital with you for identification. Use a long, forked stick and cut the snake's head off, remembering that reflex action means a snake can still bite after death. Heroics however are absurd and a good description will do as well if you don't fancy yourself as a snake hunter.

Puff adder: It is found in most places and therefore accounts for the majority of bites. It is short and fat (rarely longer than 90 cm) with a flattened almost triangular head. Its basic colour varies from a patterned grey-brown to sandy brown with a series of lighter coloured V-markings along the back and a yellow belly with black blotches. The poison is potent and locally tissue destructive. Do not tourniquet. Bathe in cold water and inject serum away from the bite.

Gaboon viper: It is found only in the forests of the Eastern Highlands. 90 to 120 cm long and stout, it has a highly patterned back in different shades of brown. The head is arrow-shaped and plain fawn and there are a series of fawn oblongs along the spine. The viper's bite is lethal. Serum must be given at once, and you may have to use adrenalin to counter severe shock.

Egyptian cobra: This is very common up to altitudes of about 1500 metres. It grows to 2 metres or so long and is dark grey-brown with a light belly and a dark band across the neck. The young are a yellowy colour with a dark band, and a variant, the Banded cobra, retains the yellow as an adult with dark bands right along the body. The head is short and pointed, with small eyes. If cornered it will raise its head and spread a wide hood before striking. Its venom attacks the nervous system with few immediate effects, but the bite will result in progressive paralysis and eventually lead to heart and lung failure. Use a tourniquet and administer serum.

Spitting cobra: Usually found in low-lying areas. It is normally between 90 and 120 cm long and is thinner than the Egyptian cobra, with a long, narrow head. It is usually a light grey-brown, sometimes with black-edged scales, and a salmon-pink or yellowish belly and has a series of irregular dark stripes like a bar code across the neck. It spits its venom at the face and is accurate to about 3 metres. Unless it gets your eyes or an open wound, all you should need to do is wash with disinfectant. If your eyes are hit, wash them out with plain water followed by a 1:4 solution of serum in water, then bandage while going for help. If it actually bites, treat as you would for an Egyptian cobra.

There are also forest cobras and rinkals in the Eastern Highlands which are similarly dangerous.

Black mamba: This is really greyish green to olive brown, its name coming from the inside of its mouth which is a deep blue-black. It is usually found at altitudes below 1500 metres and is at home either in trees or on the ground. It is long, 2 to 3 metres, slender and agile. The head is long, straight and narrow and has a poorly developed hood. Its bite affects the nervous system and can be lethal if the specific serum for mambas isn't injected very soon afterwards.

Green mamba: A rarer and smaller snake, it is usually about 150 cm long and thin. It is a tree dweller, mainly found in the Eastern Highlands. It is all one colour ranging from blue-green to a leaf green and has a long, straight, narrow head. The poison is less potent than that of the black mamba, but the effect and treatment are identical.

Boomslang: This is another tree dweller that is common throughout the country and is often mistaken for the green mamba. It is usually around 120 cm long but can go up to 180 cm. It is slender with a short head and large eyes and can vary from blue-green to leaf green, occasionally with black-edged scales. The young are a purplish-grey and the females become a greeny brown with a fawn belly. It will puff out its throat when annoyed. It is very poisonous but will usually only inject small amounts of venom. This attacks the blood, breaking down the clotting mechanism, and results in copious and prolonged bleeding. There can be up to 12 hour's delay before the symptoms appear, so there should be plenty of time to get to a doctor. The serum is rare and can only be obtained by a doctor if there is definite identification of the snake. Meanwhile avoid bumps and bruises and don't bandage tightly.

Vine snake: There are lots of these around, but they are well camouflaged and rarely seen. It grows to about 140 cm long, with a thin, tapered body and is ash grey with irregular black and white bars across the body. The head is long and pointed, green above, grey at the sides and with an orange streak from the eye to the nostril. The venom is potent, but it isn't terribly accurate so will rarely bite badly. Treat as you would for a boomslang.

Python: It is found in most areas, especially in the low veld and near water. It eats anything from mice to small buck, and a large meal can last up to a year. It will normally be between 3 and 4.5 metres but has been known to reach 6 metres. The colouring is olive with light sandy patches, and it has an elongated, spear-shaped head and little eyes. It is not poisonous and will not attack humans, though it may bite if trapped. Disinfectant should be sufficient to cure this. It is a protected species.

Big but fairly harmless

Game Viewing

To be a successful game spotter takes eagle eyes, endless patience and a taste for early rising. Get up before the sun so that by the time the light is beginning to change you will be ready to move. This is the time when the animals are about, stretching, yawning, going for an early morning drink or hunting. This is when the lions kill. Then go home for a late breakfast and spend a lazy day by the pool. All the animals will be doing the same and you won't see much in the heat of the day. Head out again at about four.

How best to go? If you have your own car you can stay out as long as you like but you will have the disadvantage, if you are in a normal saloon, of being very close to the ground and unable to see over the long grass at the side of the road.

Advantages of a tour

Tours are usually good value as the guides are trained, so are better game spotters than you and can tell you something about what you are looking at. They often keep in touch by radio with other groups, so will be able to home in on any especially exciting find.

If possible, go on a tour in an open Land Rover

49

rather than in a van or truck. You are out in the open air with the smells as well as the sights of the wild and the visibility is far better. You will also probably be able to leave the road and head right into the middle of the herds. Also go on a night tour. There is a totally different feeling about the bush after dark. The antelope and zebras move out into the open to lie on the warmer grass, the space giving them a degree of safety from predators as they sleep. And a whole new range of animals comes out, jackals and genets, antbears and scrub hares.

Walking and riding
If you have time, go on a walking or riding tour. These are always small groups conducted by an armed guard, and although you only go a short distance you can get closer to the animals than you would ever have dreamed was possible. If you are on horseback you don't smell of human and the animals will not be alarmed as you approach.

Or you can spend time in a hide. Unless you are extraordinarily lucky you won't see a vast number of different species, but it is hypnotically **Up a tree** peaceful. I spent three hours on my own up a tree at Bumi, and once I had stopped worrying about the nasties that might be sharing the hide with me I found myself watching a nearby elephant so intently that I saw every mouthful and every swish of his ears.

Wildlife to Look Out for

This is only a very short list of those animals and birds which you are most likely or would most like to see, and does not include most of the smaller or rarer species in the country. Zimbabwe's wildlife is so extensive that no definitive list has yet been compiled.

The monkey family
The monkey family includes:
Vervet and samango monkeys: You would be hard put to miss these, scattered as they are along roads, around camp sites and many houses. They are so

used to visitors that they will shamelessly steal any food left lying around. The vervet is the most common and is the smaller of the two, with a blue skin, speckled grey coat and white front, black face and white ring of whiskers. The samango is found only in the forests of the Eastern Highlands and has a whitish skin and dark blue-grey fur.

Baboons: These are much larger, weighing up to 35 kg, with grey-brown fur and square, dog-like muzzles. They live in large colonies. Their wrinkled, anxious-old-men babies ride either clinging under the mother's stomach or jockey-style on the back. Baboons are very strong, with powerful teeth, and while they will not normally attack should be treated with caution.

Bushbaby and night ape: Not technically apes, these two creatures are both common nocturnal tree-dwellers. Both are light grey with woolly fur, huge eyes and ears and have a sobbing call like a baby's cry. The only easy way of distinguishing them is by size. The bushbaby is up to 75 cm long and weighs about 1 kg. The night ape is much smaller at about 40 cm long and weighs only 170 grams.

Plains animals   Common plains animals include:

Blue wildebeeste: This belongs to the gnu family and is common throughout Africa—it is famous for its massive migrations across the Serengeti plains. An ungainly creature, it looks like a composite of several others. It is a dark silvery grey with darker brownish bands on the neck and shoulders and has a beard, mane and long, horse-like tail. Both sexes have thick, short horns, similar to a buffalo's. It has a large head and stocky neck and shoulders which slope away to narrower, more graceful hindquarters. The blue wildebeeste is usually a grazer and is very gregarious, living in large herds.

Buffalo: This is one of the largest and most ferocious of African animals though it will usually behave—and look—like a domestic cow. It has a smooth, shiny black coat, huge horns that meet over the forehead like a Viking helmet, and floppy, downturned ears. It is a herd animal, often congregating in huge numbers, and usually grazes, though it will sometimes browse on mopane bush.

Giraffe: These extraordinary creatures, with their elongated necks, can grow as high as 6 metres and are already about 2 metres tall when born. They are basically an orangy tan with brown splodges, although the markings can vary quite considerably. Their necks have only seven vertebrae (the same as other mammals) and their thigh bones are shorter than man's. Both sexes have curious antenna-like knobbed horns though the male's are slightly thicker. They have a slow-motion, rocking-horse gallop, never lie down to sleep and when drinking slowly spread their front legs and buckle at the knees before bending forward to the water. Their powerful kick is their only defence, but a fully grown adult is too large for most predators to tackle. They feed on young acacia trees.

Zebra: The size of a pony, the zebra always looks sleek and well fed, its black and white stripes sometimes shadowed by others of a yellowy brown. They have short tufted manes and small rounded ears and flowing tails. They normally congregate in large numbers and graze in the open, often mixed in with herds of antelope. They can be cross-bred with either horses or donkeys and have been tamed in the past, though this is rare.

Warthog: These incredibly ugly pig-like creatures are some of my favourites. They have a grey skin with coarse grey-brown hair, tufted whiskers around the mouth and behind the eyes and warty lumps on the face. The male has large downturned tusks that cross over the nose. They normally live in nuclear families of two adults and three babies and when alarmed will run stretched out in a line, their tails erect like flags. They feed by day on roots and grass.

Bushpig: These ferocious creatures are rarely seen as they are nocturnal, spending the day in the long grass or reeds. A fully grown adult weighs over 90 kg and has a long down-turned snout and small tusks. They are a dark reddish-brown with white on the head and mane and a black belly and legs. Piglets have yellow stripes. They eat roots, fruit, snakes, insects and eggs and are hated by farmers as expert crop raiders.

The dog family and hyenas   Dog-like creatures include:

Wild dog: These once used to hunt in packs of 50 or 60 but are rarely now seen in groups of more than 12. They are fearsome looking beasts with mottled, spotted or banded yellow, black and white markings, black muzzles, white tails and long rounded ears. They are large with long thin legs and have only four toes per foot. Don't get in their way.

Bat-eared fox: Small, dainty creatures usually found in the west of the country in packs of up to 14, they have dark grey bodies, black faces, black-tipped tails and very large ears. They are insect eaters, harmless and nocturnal.

Jackal: From a distance they look rather like Alsatians. The commonest variety, the black-backed, has a reddish head, sides and legs, well marked black and white patches along the back and a bushy black-tipped tail. The side-striped is similar but has a white tip on its tail. Jackals will occasionally go after small game, but are usually scavengers, rooting through dustbins and wreaking havoc in hen houses. They have a high pitched yap.

Spotted hyena: They are large, with a big head, small rounded ears, a short dark muzzle and powerful jaws. They have powerful shoulders but their backs slope downwards to weak back legs. They are a tawny colour with darker spotting and mottling, whitish bellies and inside legs and a short neck mane. They always look unkempt. Though usually scavengers living on carrion, they will also go after sick or injured animals. It is said that they like the smell of soap and any left lying outside the camp will be taken. Their cry is an eery hollow howl.

Big cats   Most commonly seen cats include:

Lion: They live in prides of up to 20 with one or two males surrounded by females and young. Fully grown they are about 90 cm at the shoulder and

The king of beasts at ease

weigh around 180 kg. The males make a lot of noise, usually to stampede nearby animals, but the females do most of the work, hunting at first light or dusk and spending their days in the shade.

Leopard: These are widespread, generally liking wooded country, but thanks to the skin trade they are now extremely rare. As they are also nocturnal and solitary, you will be extremely lucky if you see one in the wild. They are climbers, so look in the trees as well as below. Leopards are magnificent creatures, with large, powerful bodies and comparatively short legs. Their skin is loose, a rich gold with dark spots in groups of five like pug marks. They have rounded ears, huge round amber eyes and very long tails. The leopard has a bark like a dry cough—very similar to a baboon's.

Cheetah: It is very similar in colouring to the leopard and is often confused, particularly when it is sitting down, but it is slightly paler and has single spots instead of clusters. The face is small and almost triangular, with deep black lines running from the eyes to the mouth like the tracks of a clown's tears. The inside of the mouth and tongue are black. The ears are small and round. Once it stands up there can be no confusion, as the legs are longer and thinner and the body has almost a whippet's aerodynamic lines. They stand about 85 cm at the shoulder and weigh up to 58 kg. Speed is their main weapon and over short distances they are the fastest creatures on earth. Speeds of up to 112 kph have been recorded over a distance of 400 metres. They are solitary and are now also extremely rare. They hunt at dawn and dusk.

Smaller cats There are also several small cats which you may see at dusk: the *civet*, which is about the size of a large mog, with whitish fur, dark spots and a black-ringed tail; the *genet*, about the same size, but with a long body, short legs and a pointed face (sort of dachshund-shaped), coloured greyish-white with either brick-red or dark grey spots and a black ringed tail; the *serval*, mainly found in the east of the country, which is about 90 cm long, a light orange colour with black spots and lines and a ringed tail; and the rare *caracal*, which is a plain brick-red with a black ring round each eye and long black ears with a pointed tuft of hair on top.

The big mammals Giant mammals include:

Elephant: The African elephant is the largest of all land mammals in the world. A full grown bull can be up to 3.3 metres tall at the shoulder, weigh about 6 tonnes and have tusks up to 2.4 metres long. Pregnancy lasts a year, weaning is at five years, sexual maturity is reached at 15 and life expectancy is between 60 and 70 years. Elephants are usually browsers, ripping off whole branches or even uprooting small trees but will also graze occasionally. They have a reputation for ferocity but will rarely be troubled by your presence. If you get between a mother and baby or meet a rogue male (these have usually been banished from the herd,

Square lipped rhino at Kyle National Park

so will be alone), watch out. They flap their ears
to keep cool, so this cannot necessarily be taken
as a sign of anger, but stay alert for a change of
mood. Physical differences between the African
and Indian elephant: the African is larger, with bigger ears, has a flat forehead, a ringed trunk, a con-
cave back and it carries its head higher. Zimbabwe's
herds are so successful that the national parks have
to cull several thousand animals every now and
then to stop them turning the parks into waste-
lands.

Rhinoceros: The *black rhino* is the smaller of the two
varieties to be found in Africa. Its natural skin colour is a dark yellowy-brown though it is normally
mud-stained to a dark grey, and it has folds of loose
skin on the neck and upper legs. It is a solitary
creature, living in thick bush, and is notoriously
bad-tempered. The *white rhino* was shot out at the
end of the last century but has been reintroduced
artificially to the country with great success. It is
really the same colour as the black rhino, its name

coming from the Afrikaans word 'weit', which means wide. A more accurate name is the square-lipped rhino. This square jaw is the only 'easy' way of telling it apart from the black rhino, although I have never been able to see the difference. These are more sociable animals, living in small family groups, are larger, slower-moving and more placid. They are also grazers and live on the open plains, so you are more likely to see them. Zimbabwe's herds are again under severe threat, this time from poachers after rhino horn, a commodity infinitely more precious than gold.

Hippopotamus: You will rarely see a hippo on land during the day as they are night feeders, though there is plenty of evidence of their passing down near the water—large boggy areas of closely cropped grass and muddy wallows. During the day they will find a comfortable patch of water and huddle in groups, only their pink-rimmed nostrils showing above the water. With patience and a good pair of binoculars you will eventually see them move, rearing out of the water to stretch or give cavernous pink yawns. Hippos are smaller than rhinos with a smoother, dark grey skin and no horns. Treat them with respect. Although herbivores, those massive mouths can do, and have done, a lot of damage to humans.

The big reptile   Another big creature, this time a reptile:

Crocodile: Though these can grow up to 6 metres long, it is rare to see one above 4 metres these days. They are hatched at only a few centimetres long and are at first olive in colour with black blotches. As they get older they become a uniform black or dark olive. Starting as insect eaters, they progress through fish to mammals and become highly dangerous. They spend most of their days basking on sandbanks or in shallows, pretending to be logs, their jaws gaping to provide air conditioning. The *Nile crocodile* is the only species to be found in Zimbabwe.

Antelope you   Among antelope found in Zimbabwe are:
may see   *Bushbuck*: This is a forest dweller, found widely but

extremely shy and with excellent camouflage. Both sexes are a reddish brown, although the female is lighter in colour, and have white stripes across the back, white spots along the sides and a crest of white hair along the spine. A fully grown ram will stand up to 70 cm at the shoulder. Only males have twisted horns which can be up to 38 cm long.

Duiker: This is the smallest of the Zimbabwe antelope, not standing much higher than your knee. It is a very shy creature, its name meaning 'diver' in Afrikaans after the way it dives for cover, but it is widespread and common. The colour can vary from blue grey to fawn, with black marks on the front legs and the top of the tail. The face is a bright tan with darker patches on the forehead and cheeks and a black streak running up the nose. The male has short, straight black horns. Duikers normally live alone or in pairs, only coming out to browse at night. They are occasionally kept as pets in rural areas.

Eland: The largest of the local antelope, the eland stands up to 2 metres at the shoulder and weighs up to one tonne. It is a sandy colour with dimly marked stripes across the flat back and has a brown patch on the forehead. Both males and females have spiral horns, although the male's are much larger. The eland can jump up to 3 metres. Several farms have been set up in recent years cultivating the eland both for its milk and meat.

Impala: This is the most common of all the country's antelope, found on most open savannah land, usually in large herds. Impala are very pretty creatures with reddish brown backs fading into a white belly. The tail has a black line on the upper side and a white tip and the buttocks are white, with a black line running down each side. Females, which are hornless, have a brown patch on the top of their heads. Males have long, lyre-shaped horns. They weigh up to about 72 kg, are spectacular jumpers, making leaps up to 3 metres high and 9 metres long, and are very swift, with speeds of up to 96 kph being recorded.

Kudu: These large animals have powerful shoulders, humped necks and sloping hindquarters. They are fawn-grey with between seven and ten faint white stripes across the back, a white V on the nose, and large ears. The males have huge, curly horns up to 1.5 metres long. Females and young gather in smallish herds but males are often solitary. Kudus are browsers and shy.

Reedbuck: This antelope feeds in early morning or late afternoon near water, usually in groups of two or three. Reedbucks are a fawny grey with white necks, bellies, and inside legs. The front legs are a darker brown while the back legs have darker patches. Only the male has horns, up to 30 cm long, curling forward and out from a soft growing pad.

Sable: This magnificent animal has been adopted as the national emblem of Zimbabwe. A fully grown bull will stand about 1.4 metres at the shoulder and has a shiny black coat. The female is slightly smaller and lighter in colour. Both have white bellies, white striped faces and enormous horns that sweep back in a clean curve, measuring up to 1.5 metres in length. They are gregarious creatures, living in herds of up to 60, grazing on open grassland in the early morning and late afternoon.

Waterbuck: Another largish, fairly solidly built antelope, the waterbuck is usually found in small groups near water. The coat is a uniform fawny grey and the most distinguishing mark is a white circle on the buttocks. Only the males have large horns.

Birds of Zimbabwe

Birds you may see in Zimbabwe include:

Cattle egret: These pure white birds have a slender profile, short, straight beak and tufted crest. They are usually found anywhere there are large herds, either domestic or wild, perching on the animals' backs or running under their feet to grab the insects disturbed as they pass. They always live in large colonies and are often mistakenly called tick birds. The true tick bird is the small, brown and far less noticeable *oxpecker*.

Crowned crane: These magnificent birds live in pairs

on open land near water. They are tall, elegant and slender with grey backs, brown tails, white wings and black legs. The neck is white and the head black with white cheeks and an orange patch under the beak. The crowning glory is a large golden crest. They have a booming call and complicated mating rituals that involve dancing, wings outspread. The crowned crane is not common but is worth looking out for.

Fish eagle: One of the few eagles still found reasonably frequently, these are mainly fish eaters but will also take small mammals. They are heavy birds with a white head and breast, black wings and thick black legs. They have a small, hooked beak and a raucous triple cry. Look for them perched on the high branches of dead trees.

Grey heron: Usually found alone, near open water, these are large, pale grey birds with darker patches on the underside of the wings and head and long, straight beaks. They have a hunch-backed appearance when standing still and utter a guttural cry on taking off.

Helmeted guinea fowl: These ground dwellers live in large, noisy flocks. They have small dark heads and round ungainly bodies that are basically brown, covered with a mass of faint blue spots. This is the only game bird in Zimbabwe to be eaten regularly.

Hornbills: There are two species commonly found in Zimbabwe, the *grey or tree hornbill* which is the smaller of the two, grey with dappled dark grey spots and white front, and the much larger browny red and black *ground hornbill* which is mainly a ground dweller but will also fly for short distances. Both have huge, down-turned beaks similar to the toucan's, and ungainly flight and loud, trumpeting calls.

Mzilikaze's roller: Commonly known as blue jays, these small, pretty birds live singly or in pairs but are usually to be found in fairly large numbers away from urban areas, often perched along phone lines, on dead branches, etc. The chest, neck and the top of the wings are orange, the lower underside and underneath the wings pale blue, and the top of the head white. They have harsh, rasping voices and acrobatic flight.

Ostrich: These massive birds are Zimbabwe's only truly flightless bird, their powerful kick and great height giving them the protection they need as adults. The black and white male is best known and in most demand for its feathers. The female is slightly smaller and a dull brown in colour. They live either in pairs or small flocks of one male and two or three females and can usually be found out in open savannah country. Male and female share the responsibility of incubating the eggs and bringing up the young. They are farmed both for their meat and feathers.

Secretary bird: Technically a species of eagle, these peculiar birds look more like cranes, with slim bodies, long spindly legs and small heads. They are mostly pale grey, with dark legs, tail and underside of wings. The short hooked beak is orange. They are normally found on the ground where their main diet is snakes, though they also eat smaller rodents. Their name drives both from their subdued colouring and the dark crest that sticks up like a bunch of quill pens.

Glossy starling: There are several species of this very common and very gregarious bird, all nearly identical. About the same size as a European starling, the glossy starling is a uniform deep sea blue that changes in the light like shot silk from turquoise to black.

Weaver birds: You are more likely to see their colonies than the birds themselves as most bare trees in rural areas of Zimbabwe are festooned with the nests of the sociable weaver bird. There are several species in the country, all small (around the size of a sparrow) and yellow. The most common is the masked weaver, which has a black head. The same colonies are used year after year, their hanging nests being repaired and enlarged as required.

Vultures: There are several species of vultures and

carnivorous storks in the country, huge, ungainly birds with shaggy feathers and bald heads. They may well be seen anywhere there has been or is likely to be a kill.

There are also many species of *doves*, *ducks*, *kingfishers* and *hoopoes* as well as a wide variety of other birds, both indigenous and migratory.

HISTORICAL BACKGROUND

Prehistory

The earliest humanoid skeletons found in southern
Africa have been classified as Australopithicenes,
tiny people (up to 130 cm tall and weighing no more
than 32 kilos) who lived between about five million
and 850,000 years ago. They are thought to be one
of the earliest links in the history of man but what
happened during the millions of years of their exis-
tence and the succeeding millenia is pretty much
a blur, the little that is known being pieced together
from tiny, far-flung fragments of bone. It is not
until about 70,000 years ago that regular evidence
of the use of rudimentary tools begins to offer
further clues. At about this time too, fire was discovered and those living on the fringes of the savannah and forest turned to eating meat.

**Homo sapiens
in southern
Africa**
By 50,000 years ago, southern Africa's inhabitants, now classified as Homo sapiens (Boskopoid)
and thought to be the direct ancestors of the bushmen, were moving to the watersheds and the
denser forest, using fire and traps for hunting, and
other materials such as bone, skin, wood and
sinew.

Another relatively static period followed until,
about 12,000 years ago, the Magosian people
appeared throughout sub-Saharan Africa, bringing
with them a new, greatly more skilled type of
stonework that used microliths, or tiny flakes of
stone, wood or bone to make more complex
composite weapons.

Desert barrier
10,000 years ago the climate changed, getting
much drier. People began to wander in search of
food and water, creating an explosion of knowledge
and civilisation throughout Europe, Africa and
Asia, only brought to a halt in Africa when the
Sahara spread to form an almost impassable barrier.
An ever widening gap began to grow in the way
the peoples of Africa and Europe developed,

63

Australopithecus hunted small game in the grasslands of southern Africa

although African society by no means fossilised as some would claim. From about 8000 years ago formal tribal social organisation appeared with laws, institutions and ceremonies. And although still nomadic, Africa's inhabitants also began to specialise, producing a far wider range of material goods of an increasingly better standard, travelling enormously long distances in a complex web of trade and barter.

Cave paintings

It is during this period that we find the first of the Bushman cave paintings. None of the earliest, thought to be purely ceremonial, survive today. Of those that can still be seen, the oldest are naturalistic pictures of local animals or hunting scenes. A little later they begin to chart the peaceful arrival of new peoples, probably the Hottentots or Bantu. Later still, the quality of the work drops off dramatically, and is thought to be copy-cat work by a different race.

The Bantu

In about 300 BC, negro and Hamitic people (who had recently discovered the use of iron) started moving south ahead of the spreading Sahara. They seem to have been welcomed and certainly intermarried, for most of Africa's people today (except for a tiny number of surviving bushmen and pygmies) are part of the resulting Bantu group. The Bantu (meaning man) are not one people, having an enormous variety of physical characteristics and skin colourings, and are really only connected by language. By AD 300 iron was being worked in southern Africa by a people christened the Gokomere by archaeologists. By AD 500 they had settled an area stretching from the Nyanga Highlands to the Transvaal and northeast Botswana. They are also thought to be the first inhabitants of Great Zimbabwe, being joined there later by two more groups, with whom they seem to have lived peacefully.

First inhabitants of Great Zimbabwe

In about AD 1000, however, another new people arrived, thought to be the Karanga or early Shona. They too seem to have lived peacefully at first, introducing spinning and weaving and trading for gold with the coastal Arabs. But by the end of the 11th C, competition for hunting and grazing land seemed to be growing fierce and the first fortifications were being built.

Arab traders had arrived in East Africa in about 600 BC, gradually spreading further south to create a major trading post at Sofala on the Mozambique coast. A Greek navigator of the 1st C AD wrote of

The royal quarters at Great Zimbabwe

trade with the interior in wax and ivory, tortoise shell, rhino horn and palm oil. Arab accounts, together with archaeological evidence and oral traditions, finally begin to give a reasonably clear picture of what the early Shona kingdoms were like, although it was not until the 15th C that the written record provides any real detail.

The Shona

The Shona were in fact made up of several tribes, chief amongst them the Karanga and the Rozwi, who came from the north, subduing other tribes and creating a series of vassal states even before they reached Zimbabwe. From the 11th to the 15th C they thrived, a relatively peaceful, monotheistic society, worshipping a deity called Mwari, and relegating the bushmen to slave status.

It was the Golden Age of Great Zimbabwe, built round a shrine to Mwari on the acropolis (Mwanha Hill). Here an empire was gradually built up that would catch the imagination of the outside world, firing Europeans even into the 19th C with jealousy for its supposedly fabulous wealth. The reality was not as romantic.

The Rozwi were ruled by a Mambo, heriditary head of a powerful, probably priestly family, who took semi-divine status from his position as sole communicator with the ancestral spirits (mhondoro). Surrounded by an elaborate court ritual, commoners could only address him from a prostrate position, their faces averted, slowly clapping and speaking through an intermediary. He held absolute power of life and death, and the well-being of the entire country was synonymous with that of his personal health.

Mwene Mutapa

In about 1450, Mambo Mutota led an empire-building raid against the Tavara tribe who named him Mwene Mutapa (Great Plunderer), a title (later corrupted by the Europeans to Monomotapa) he kept and passed to his heirs. By the time of his death later in 1450, he controlled the whole area from the Limpopo to the Zambezi. His son Matope moved the capital to Fura Mountain near Mazowe and all was peaceful until about 1490 when Changa, Matope's son by a slave wife and governor of Guruhuswa province (centred on Great Zimbabwe), attacked Matope's successor, Nyahuma, with the help of Arab traders, killed him and took power. Around four years later, Nyahuma's son regained independence, but the Mwene Mutapa had lost forever the centre and south of the kingdom which stayed in the hands of Changa (who now took the title of Changamire).

So when the first Europeans arrived in the early 16th C, taking home exaggerated reports of Solomon's 'Land of Ophir', great empires and mountains of gold, power was already split between the

Mwene Mutapa at Fura and the Changamire at Zimbabwe and both were becoming figureheads as local rulers gathered real power into their own hands. Gold was being mined solely as a way of feeding voracious traders and ensuring a regular supply of cloth, beads and other luxuries. The once-great empire was crumbling.

The Portuguese

Vasco da Gama In 1497 Vasco da Gama rounded the Cape of Good Hope and became the first European to reach the East African coast, opening up new possibilities of trade to the Portuguese, confirmed on his third voyage in 1502 when he stopped at Sofala, discovered the gold trade and heard rumours of magnificent wealth.

In 1514, Antonio Fernandez was sent inland to check these out. He made two journeys, during which time he wrote the first detailed accounts of Shona society, and recommended the area as being suitable for Europeans to live in. Nothing, however, was done until 1560, when a Jesuit priest, **The first** Father Gonçalo Silveira, was given permission to **European in** visit Fura Mountain. On arrival, he was greeted **Zimbabwe** as an honoured guest and offered gold, cattle and slaves. Being ignorant of local custom, he refused them and deeply offended the Mwene Mutapa. Undaunted, he tried to set up a mission but again offended sensibilities and was eventually ordered to leave the kingdom. When he refused he was put to death together with 50 recent converts. His martyr's death created a wave of enthusiasm for missionary work in Europe, not shared on the whole by the local missionaries.

In 1565, King Sebastiano of Portugal decided to take over all African territory south of the Zambezi, and in 1569 sent Francisco de Barreto out as first independent governor of Portuguese East Africa. Barreto took a huge formal expedition into the interior. The Mwene Mutapa eventually agreed to meet only if the Portuguese would help him defeat Chikanga, chief of the Manyika, who was threatening his position. They agreed and fought Chikanga at Nyanga. Neither side won definitely, but the Portuguese, shaken by the encounter, gave up and went back to the coast.

In 1571 Fernandez Homem, the new governor, tried again and reached Chikanga's mines near the Vumba. He had expected to find great nuggets lying around ready to be picked up, and disillusioned by what he found, he too went back to the coast after negotiating a trade treaty. Little more was done until the end of the century when, in **Traders and** 1596, Mwene Mutapa Gatsi Rusere asked the Portu- **missionaries** guese for military aid, offering them mining and trading concessions in return. In 1607 both the Jesuits and Dominicans went inland again. This time the Jesuits survived until the order was quashed by the Marquis of Pombal in 1759. The Dominicans lasted until 1775 when they were recalled to Goa, only returning a century later during the great missionary resurgence that included such people as Livingstone and the London Missionary Society.

From 1607 onwards, the Portuguese began to interfere more and more in the empire's internal politics in spite of growing resentment. In 1629 Mwene Mutapa Kapararidze tried to get rid of all foreigners and for a short while it looked as if he had succeeded. By 1630 there were only five left in his territory and seven in Chikanga's. But in 1632, Diego da Meneses retaliated, burning Chikanga's village, killing Kaparatidze, and setting up a puppet, Mavura, who became a Portuguese vas- **Portuguese** sal and gave them wide trading and unlimited min- **dominion...** ing rights. He also agreed to build churches and allow the missionaries free rein. Future Mwene Mutapas were all to be baptised and could no longer demand court formalities from Portuguese officials. A Portuguese 'Captain of the Gate' was set up at a trading post, Masape, near Fura Mountain to regulate all trade with the kingdom.

This Portuguese stranglehold lasted for several decades, but eventually it began to crumble due to rampant corruption. A resentful Mutapa asked the Changamire to help and in 1693 Changamire attacked the Portuguese settlement at Damarare, massacring its inhabitants. Other raids followed and by the turn of the century the Portuguese had again left the plateau, this time for good.

and expulsion

The Zulus

Zimbabwe's gold trade tapered off to a mere trickle, the empire was totally fragmented, and there was little real power left amongst the ruling classes.

By the late 18th C the Bantu peoples stretched most of the way across present-day South Africa, a peaceful people with a loosely knit tribal network, until in 1780, Dingiswayo, chief of the Mtetwa clan, decided to unite them all under his rule. He did so rapidly and by force, setting up a formidable army to police the federation.

Shaka creates the Zulu war machine

In 1800 he was killed by a young captain, Shaka, from the insignificant Zulu clan, who took over, changing the name of the whole tribe to Zulu, and refining his military techniques to form a terrifying fighting force that ruled through fear. This reign of terror produced a backlash and 20 years of bloodshed followed, stripping huge areas of land bare of inhabitants.

The Ndebele settle in Zimbabwe

Mzilikaze, the son of a rebel captain put to death by Shaka, fled north with his followers, the Ndebele, eventually crossing the Limpopo and settling in the Bulawayo area in 1838. They lived by raiding along the borders of their territory, terrifying the local Shona population who took to living in hidden caves or paying to be left in peace. By the time the British arrived in the 1870s, Mzilikaze's son, Lobengula, had again created a legend of fabulous wealth. To this day tales still abound of his lost treasure and the fortune waiting for anyone who can find it. In the late 19th C it was sufficient to fuel the gold-based greed of the colonists.

The Explorers

By the mid-19th C England was beginning to take an interest in southern Africa, although only a few missionaries and traders strayed north of the Limpopo. In 1840 the young David Livingstone arrived at the London Missionary Society's mission at Kuruman, spending ten years there and marrying Robert Moffat's daughter Mary. But he was always **Livingstone's** restless and adventurous and longed to head north. **discovery of** In 1849, he was given permission and two years **the Zambezi** later discovered the Zambezi, a great highway which could be a route right across the heart of Africa. Following this dream, he reached the west coast at Luanda before backtracking to go downstream, reaching the Mozambique coast at Quelimane in 1855. His journey was a feat which justified a hero's welcome on his return to England.

'Neither civilisation nor Christianity can be promoted alone. In fact they are inseparable', he claimed, handing the missionaries their justification for helping the commercially-based colonists— and imbuing the colonists with a purer motive than greed.

From God rush Livingstone's reports spurred the London Mis- **to gold rush** sionary Society into action, and Robert Moffat obtained permission from Mzilikazi, an old friend, to start a mission near his capital at Inyati. In 1859 he went north together with his son John Smith Moffat and two other English families.

In 1870, Mzilikazi died and was succeeded by his son, Lobengula, who moved his capital to Bulawayo. John Smith Moffat was given permission to open a second mission here. They made no conversions but the missionaries became invaluable to the king as interpreters and advisers.

Meantime, ivory traders had also begun to move north. In 1865 three of them, Viljoen, Hartley and Jacobs went into Mashonaland and found the old gold workings, and in 1867 Karl Mauch, who was also a geologist, reported back on the gold potential of Matabeleland. Rumours began to fly and when, in 1873, he discovered Great Zimbabwe, prospectors disappointed in the South African gold rush began flooding north.

Rhodes

Cecil Rhodes arrived in Kimberley in 1871 and by a mixture of hard bargaining, shrewd business sense and courage soon created the fortune that was to provide the means for his future actions. Money however was little more than a game to him and when he returned to Oxford in 1873, he was looking for a greater purpose. He found it in the speeches of two men, Ruskin and Froude, who were preaching of a great colonial commonwealth, providing sun and space for all Britain's masses. To their theories Rhodes added a little half-baked Darwinism to convince himself that the English represented the pinnacle of civilisation and that it was their Christian duty to create a global society of justice, peace and liberty.

He returned to South Africa permanently in 1881 and was elected to the Cape Parliament. Before long **Dream of a** he was looking north, dreaming of a railway run-**Cape to Cairo** ning from Cape Town to Cairo, preferably through **railway** British territory the whole way. He had to move fast. The Germans had recently moved into German South-West Africa (Namibia) and the Boers were talking of moving into the northern land. When in 1887 Kruger signed a treaty with Lobengula providing for a permanent Boer representative at his court, Rhodes finally managed to persuade the Cape Parliament to act. They took over Southern Bechuanaland as a Crown Colony and North Bechuanaland as a British Protectorate and John Moffat was instructed to tell Lobengula that the Boer treaty was invalid. Trusting his old friend, Lobengula signed a new treaty in February 1888 promising perpetual friendship with Great Britain and agreeing not to deal with any other power without British consent.

From now on the story becomes one of lies, duplicity and trickery. Lobengula had never before dealt with European politics and papers. He realised he could not refuse to deal, but had little idea of what was really at stake. More importantly, he lived by a code of honour which meant not only that his own promises were inviolate but that he trusted impicitly those with whom he was dealing.

In September 1888 Rhodes sent the king a private message asking for a concession to all mineral rights in his kingdom. Lobengula was immediately tempted. One concession would get rid of the ever-increasing number of private prospectors cluttering up his country, and all his advisers, including Moffat, urged him to accept the deal. He signed. He and his heirs would receive £100 a month, 1000 breach-loading rifles and 10,000 rounds of ammunition, and a steamer for the Zambezi. Rhodes was to get 'complete and exclusive charge over all minerals and metals... together with full power to do all things they may deem necessary... to procure the same'.

Rhodes swindles the king

It didn't take long for the king to start regretting the deal and in January 1889, Rhodes' chief rival for the concession, Maund, persuaded Lobengula to send representatives to London to find out what was going on. Rhodes managed to delay them long enough for him to get there first.

The use of Charter Companies to open up land too expensive for the Crown to fund had recently been revived in East Africa and Rhodes was well received by Lord Salisbury, then Prime Minister. Here was a man who was rich enough to fund the entire operation, and build the railway north.

But he was working against the clock. He had to get the Charter signed before the news that Lobengula had rescinded the treaty could reach London. He used money, buying out his rivals, including Maund, and forming a syndicate, United Concessions, as the central core of the British South Africa Company. He then bought the Irish vote, and put the Duke of Fife, the Duke of Abercorn and Earl Grey, all eminently respectable men, on his board.

On 29 October, the Charter was granted, and, as with everything conceived by Rhodes, covered far more ground than the original concession, giving the Company what amounted to sovereign

Cecil Rhodes standing on the spot which is now his grave

rights over an area far greater than Matabeleland and Mashonaland. It was meant to be exercised only with Lobengula's approval, and under the supervision of the Secretary of State, but no official was sent out as overseer.

The Pioneers

Preparations for the pioneer column had begun as soon as the Concession was signed and 200 men were recruited, all with previous South African experience, most of them under 30. They had a wide variety of practical skills, from farming to mining and trade. Each man was to be paid 7/6 per day and on arrival would be allowed to stake out a farm of 3000 acres (1400 hectares) and up to 15 gold claims. In addition, 400 mounted men went as guard and to form the core of the British South Africa Police.

Settlement by deception Lobengula's protests grew louder, but again and again he was assured that they were only looking for minerals. When the column was finally given permission to leave however, its stated aim was 'the peaceful occupation of Mashonaland'. The column of over 100 wagons left on 27 June 1890, reaching open country and running up the flag at Fort Victoria by August. They reached Mount Hampden by September and on the 12th officially staked out the town of Fort Salisbury.

Rhodes now turned his attention to Manicaland, which was also being claimed by the Portuguese, who were quoting their ancient treaties with the Mwene Mutapa. They had already agreed a treaty with Mtasa, the most powerful chief in the area, when Jameson arrived in the district in September 1890 and overturned it, forcing Mtasa to sign a new concession giving Britain all mineral rights, a resident, police force and a school. The Portuguese sent in an army, but the settlers attacked Mtasa's village, arrested the Portuguese and set up Umtali as the Company's area headquarters. After a greal deal of further wrangling, Britain and Portugal signed

75

an agreement on 11 June 1891, settling the border along its present line.

By now Lobengula had realised quite how thoroughly he had been duped, and attempted to balance Rhodes' power by agreeing a land concession with a Johannesburg trader called Edward Lippert, not knowing that Rhodes had already agreed to buy the concession from him. In April 1891 the British High Commissioner in the Cape declared all land north of the Transvaal, between Mozambique and German South-West Africa, to be British territory and gave the BSA Company jurisdiction over all Europeans in the area. In May this was extended to include all inhabitants, black and white. Lobengula could do nothing but protest.

The British assume jurisdiction over whites and blacks

The settlers slowly entrenched their position, while Ndebele warriors massed along the border. By 1893 it seemed that war was inevitable, and while the Queen sent messages to Lobengula, assuring him of her peaceful intentions, the settlers armed. Rhodes ducked out of sight to prevent the High Commissioner from stopping him, only reappearing after the Company columns were in Matabele territory. When Lobengula moved his armies forward to block their way, a second column came up from Bechuanaland, destroying the royal kraal and forcing the king to flee. In November 1893 Bulawayo was taken over as the Company's Matabeleland headquarters. The war continued for some time and the settlers suffered several setbacks, but the contest was uneven and after Lobengula's death resistance crumpled. In 1894 a Matabele Order of Council gave the Company the same powers in Matabeleland as they already had in Mashonaland and the new country was given its name, Rhodesia, alternatives such as Rhodesland and Cecilia having been rejected. Rhodes was understandably flattered: 'Has anyone else had a country called after their name? Now I don't care what they do with me!'

The creation of Rhodesia

A Land Commission was set up, giving the Ndebele two tribal reserves, one of the Gwaai

A pioneer column

River, one at Shangani. One was short of water, the other infested by tsetse fly. The royal herds were redistributed and a large portion confiscated. The Ndebele were a proud people, and the indignities of this treatment fuelled a new wave of anger. When in 1895 a serious epidemic of rinderpest swept through the country and many of those cattle which survived it were shot in an attempt to stem the disease, their resentment boiled over. In October 1895 Jameson took all but 40 of the police with him on an abortive raid against the Kruger government in the Transvaal and the Ndebele seized their opportunity. Trouble started in March 1896, locking the settlers in the towns where they virtually starved while waiting for relief. In June the Mashona, who'd finally realised that these people, unlike the Portuguese, had come to stay and were taking their land, also rebelled.

African revolt

It was Rhodes himself who finally brought an end to the fighting, spending several days in the Matopos discussing terms with the indunas (elders). In Mashonaland the end was further away and came only after bitter conflict, but here too it was all over by the end of the year.

Development

Over the next few years the settlers dug themselves in, creating homes and farms, towns and transport. The first section of Rhodes' dream railway reached Bulawayo in 1897, and in 1898 the first train reached Umtali on the line from the Mozambique port of Beira. By 1899 this line had been extended to Salisbury. By 1902, when Rhodes died, Salisbury and Bulawayo had also been linked and the line up through Victoria Falls was nearing completion.

Railway growth

The BSAC relaxed its rules to allow individuals to stake claims, and gold output doubled. Coal and asbestos were discovered and by the outbreak of the First World War chrome and zinc were also being mined.

The settlers were most concerned however with

White land grab the land, which was sold off in vast quantities. By 1923, 74 million acres (30 million hectares) were in white hands. Those Africans already living there were encouraged to stay, to provide a workforce, and several attempts were made to force them into what amounted to little more than slave labour. The final solution was a hut tax, to be paid by all men who didn't work for at least four months of the year. Most preferred to pay than work and thousands of pounds poured into the Company coffers.

Although some areas were reserved for tribal use, the settlers kept for themselves both the lion's share and the prime land on the justification that they would make better use of it. The reserves were only to be a form of token protection and, as the Africans were to be their labour force, not a means of support. It was further decided that as productivity should increase in line with the population it would not be necessary to reconsider the position for at least 50 years.

A joint administration for Matabeleland and Mashonaland was created, headed by a Legislative Council made up of five Company appointees and four elected members. To vote you had either to own a house valued at £75 or have an income of £50 a year. Africans were not excluded but only a few hundred were eligible and as more met the qualifications, these were raised.

Breakdown of tribal authority Even in law things became more difficult for the Africans as all real power was stripped from the chiefs and all but the most trivial civil cases were heard before the local Native Commissioner. Tribal traditions began to break down and by the outbreak of the First World War little was heard of the country's black population, except as the 'Native Question'.

Responsible Government

In 1915 the Company's charter, which had been granted for a period of 25 years, expired and the interim extension contained the provision that the

SOUTHERN RHODESIA

FOR TOURIST AND SETTLER

For further information apply to —
THE SUPERINTENDENT,
Southern Rhodesia Publicity Bureau
(P.O. Box 861 BULAWAYO.)

'All this is ours'

Legislative Council could ask for Responsible Government status. Most people were agreed that Company rule should end, but there was also a strong movement backed by the Company in favour of Union with South Africa.

A referendum held in 1923 was won by the pro-Responsible Government group, however. The Company was paid almost £4 million compensation for their costs in administering the territory, giving up in return all rights except its own lands, its mineral rights and the railway. The new constitution came into effect on 1 October 1923 with a Governor and a single house of parliament with 30 members from 15 electoral districts. Elections were to be held at least every five years and a prime minister, who would rule with a cabinet of six ministers, would be chosen from the majority party. The franchise was given to all British subjects of any race with an income of over £200 a year.

The next decade was a difficult one for the fledgling state which was hit hard by the Depression, with many white families going bankrupt and surviving only with the aid of soup kitchens. The 1934 election was won by the United Party led by Godfrey Huggins, who went on to become the longest serving prime minister in the history of the Commonwealth. He immediately began a massive programme of road and bridge building to revive the economy. In 1939 Beit Bridge (across the Limpopo), Birchenough Bridge (across the Sabi) and the Otto Beit Bridge (across the Zambezi) were all completed.

Segregation policy
Huggins also thought up a new policy of 'parallel development' which stated that while both black and white communities would be allowed to develop, it must be in separate areas, and there should be no fraternising except in a master-servant relationship. Eventually the two would meet at the highest level, but this of course was seen as an event so distant as not to be worth worrying about. The policy was a popular one with the white voters; a series of acts was passed with a view to segregat-

ing the communities, such as the Native Passes Act which required all Africans to register, carry identity cards and get permission to travel, and the notorious Land Apportionment Act. It was already becoming clear that the pressure on the reserves was too great for the system to survive much longer, and while Africans had theoretically been allowed to buy land since the early 1920s they had only taken some 45,000 acres (20,000 hectares). This Act created a new class of land, Native Purchase Areas, of some 7.5 million acres (3 million hectares), to be sold only to Africans at an affordable rate. The sting in the tail was a law forbidding them to settle permanently in white areas—which included all towns.

First Stirrings

The first black political party, the Bantu Voter's Association, had been formed in the 1920s, but by 1938, as the Bantu Congress of Southern Rhodesia, it still had only 150 members. Now, slowly, things began to change and in 1945 the organisation changed its name again—to the African National Congress. In the same year there was an unofficial railway strike and in 1948 there was industrial unrest in Bulawayo and a widespread general strike. The Native Labour Board Act finally fixed minimum standards of employment and salaries for African workers, although not one black worker was paid more than a quarter of the lowest paid white worker. And it was not until 1959 that the Africans were officially given recognition of their status as employees and allowed to join a union.

In the reserves the traditional pattern of shifting cultivation was giving way to static farming and the land was being destroyed by overuse. The government started intensive training programmes and in 1951 the Native Land Husbandry Act laid aside some areas of the reserves for individual plots to be given to selected qualified farmers. The tribal system of communal ownership was finally shattered and many people were driven off the land

Growth of black trade union and political activity

which could no longer support them. The result was a bigger, more stable industrial workforce for the Europeans, but it also created a large, discontented urban community ripe for the message of the political movements which flowered in the late 1950s.

Federation

The idea of amalgamation between Northern and Southern Rhodesia and Nyasaland had first been suggested in the early 1930s, but by 1949 it was clear that this would not be allowed by the Labour Government in Britain. A federation was proposed instead. The Africans were as hostile as ever but by early 1951 agreement in principle had been given by Westminster.

In September a conference at Victoria Falls set out the basic principles of social and economic partnership between the Africans and Europeans. This principle of 'partnership' was to supersede that of 'parallel development'. Both Africans and Europeans were to recognise the rights of the other to live there, and the Europeans were to help the Africans reach an equal level. The details were vague however and no time limit was set.

In October 1951 the Conservatives returned to power in Britain and in 1953 agreed a constitution. There was to be a Governor-General and an executive council or cabinet responsible to a federal parliament of 36 members—18 from Southern Rhodesia, 11 from Northern Rhodesia and 7 from Nyasaland. Native affairs and anything else specific to one state only were to be retained by the territorial governments. There were to be two African members and one European with specific responsibility for African affairs from each country in the Federal Assembly, backed by an African Affairs Board with the power of veto over discriminatory bills. To change the constitution would require a two-thirds majority of the Assembly and Imperial approval. There was to be a review of the system in between seven and nine years.

Royal Assent was given in April 1953 and the federation was inaugurated in October, with the capital in Salisbury. A few concessions were made such as the reform of the Trade Union Law to give black workers representation, the creation of multiracial university in Salisbury, and changes in the law to let black professionals practice in the city centre and allow Africans to enter the hotels and clubs. But there was no real move towards increased black political power.

18 months later everyone began to plan towards the review. All three territorial governments wanted independence, but knew they could not get it without giving the Africans more power. Black opposition began to grow.

In March 1956, Godfrey Huggins, by now Lord Malvern, instigated a two-tiered franchise at both federal and territorial level, a system which survived in Southern Rhodesia, the future Zimbabwe, at least, until 1980. Neither roll was to be limited to one race but in practice there would be few Africans on the Upper Roll, which required electors to be property-owning British citizens. The black opposition began to demand 'one man, one vote'.

Unrest

In 1957 Joshua Nkomo, a former social worker, founded a new African National Congress (the post-war ANC was now defunct). Trouble spread throughout the federation and in February 1959 the new Prime Minister in Southern Rhodesia, Sir Edgar Whitehead, declared a state of emergency and arrested some 500 Africans. A series of bills was passed allowing the government to detain political opponents without trial for indefinite periods and the ANC was banned. By 1960 however most of the detainees had been released, and new parties, stronger, better disciplined and more militant, such as the National Democratic Party, sprang up to replace the proscribed organisations. Riots in both Salisbury and Bulawayo led to fatalities and once again the party leaders were detained, although Nkomo himself was out of the country.

Nevertheless the government was forced to make further concessions. An Education Act was passed, aiming to give all African children some education by 1964; the Trade Disputes Act created multi-racial unions; separate Post Office counters and discrimination in the betting laws were abolished; and the Urban African Housing Programme was speeded up.

The Royal Commission appointed to review the federation arrived in February 1960 and recommended that the federation remain intact while realising the need for major reforms. Amongst its proposals were a higher proportion of African seats in the Assembly, an extended franchise, decreased federal power, all discriminatory legislation to go, a Bill of Rights to guarantee equality, a new Council of State to replace the African Affairs Board and the right of any member state to secede. British Prime Minister Harold Macmillan qualified this by saying that any country must have an African-supported government before permission would be given.

Independence for Malawi (formerly Nyasaland) and Zambia (formerly Northern Rhodesia)

Both Nyasaland and Northern Rhodesia instituted new majority-based constitutions and in June 1963 a Victoria Falls conference began the break up of the federation. Malawi was promised independence in July 1964 as a Commonwealth Dominion and Zambia became a Commonwealth Republic in October 1964. Only white Southern Rhodesia was kept under British rule.

UDI

A new constitution had been agreed in Southern Rhodesia too in 1961, creating an Assembly of 65 members, 50 elected by a mainly white A roll, and 15 black and elected by the B roll. A Declaration of Rights was built in and a Constitutional Council of 12 set up to guard against discrimination. All outside control over internal affairs was to go, although British permission was still needed to alter the constitution.

In January 1961 civil service posts were opened to all races, cinemas and swimming pools were desegregated and the Immorality Act dropped, allowing mixed marriages for the first time. A few months later the Pass Laws were repealed, although Africans still had to carry identification papers, and the Land Apportionment Act was revised to allow Africans to buy freeholds in the townships. In June a further amendment created a new class of unreserved land, open to people of any race. In December however the leniency stopped when there were further, fatal riots in Salisbury, and the NDP was banned. A week later Nkomo formed the even more militant Zimbabwe African People's Union (ZAPU).

Nkomo creates ZAPU

The riots continued sporadically over the next few months and Whitehead strengthened the state of emergency, extending it for the next five years. ZAPU was banned, but this time Nkomo had had enough of changing names. He left the country and the organisation went underground.

White backlash

At the end of 1962 elections resulted in a right-wing backlash and the newly formed Rhodesian Front Party headed by Winston Field came to power. Its policies included white supremacy for the immediate future, continued land segregation and immediate independence for Southern Rhodesia.

The new government began to strip all the recent gains from the black population. In rural areas they enlisted the chiefs, whose dwindling power made them glad to cooperate, to enforce the hated land laws. Popular black movements were banned, students were forbidden to debate politics and the media were brought under government control. A mandatory death sentence was brought in for arson. In mid-1963 ZAPU split, the intellectual and radical wing breaking away to form the Zimbabwe African National Union (ZANU) headed by Ndabaningi Sithole, who was already under detention. Nkomo was detained in 1964.

Creation of ZANU

Meanwhile the cabinet also split and in April 1964 Ian Smith took over as Prime Minister, immediately beginning an outspoken campaign for independence. Eventually in October 1965 the British government laid out a series of principles to be met before independence would be granted. These were (a) unimpeded progress to majority rule, (b) guarantees against retrogressive amendments to the constitution, (c) an immediate improvement in African political status, (d) progress towards ending racial discrimination and (e) the British government to be satisfied that the basis for independence was agreeable to the people as a whole: British Prime Minister Harold Wilson, however, undermined the principles by guaranteeing that there would be no military intervention.

The whites declare independence

A state of emergency was declared on the 5 November, and on the 11 November 1965 Ian Smith made a Unilateral Declaration of Independence (UDI), paraphrasing shamelessly the 1776 American Declaration and claiming, with echoes of Livingstone, that Rhodesia had 'struck a blow for the preservation of justice, civilisation and Christianity'. A new constitution, published the same day, removed all the existing controls against apartheid.

Smith's action created shock waves round the world, African and Asian members of the United Nations began to press for action, and as the white Rhodesians had set themselves up as 'the last bastion against Communism' (a Communist being anyone slightly left-wing of the Rhodesia Front), it took on overtones of the Cold War. Britain seemed most concerned with legalities.

The failure of sanctions

On 19 November a United Nations resolution imposed diplomatic and selective economic sanctions. In a matter of weeks South Africa became a clearing house, relabelling Rhodesian goods for export and importing those foreign products needed by the Rhodesians. The pioneering white Rhodesians thrived on the adversity, seriously seeing themselves as martyred prophets crying in the wilderness.

On 17 December an oil embargo was announced, but as the Beira pipeline continued to pump and the South Africans were supplying thousands of gallons by road and rail, it was a toothless gesture. In April the UN Security Council allowed Britain to set up a naval blockade around Beira, using force if necessary.

In 1968 the United Nations had called for comprehensive mandatory sanctions but by 1971 Rhodesia's exports were above the 1965 level and, if anything, sanctions had created a dynamic new internal industry. Only foreign exchange and heavy machinery were in short supply. Talks with the British government on *HMS Tiger* in December 1965 and on *HMS Fearless* in October 1968 collapsed.

On 11 November 1968 the Union Jack was replaced by a new green and white Rhodesian flag and in June 1969 a referendum voted in favour of becoming a republic. Yet another new constitution created separate voters' rolls for Africans and Europeans with no cross-voting. The Declaration of Rights was amended so that it no longer gave legal protection and excluded any mention of preventive detention.

Apartheid reinstated
Parks, playing fields and swimming pools were again closed to Africans. The Land Tenure Act redivided the land between black and white and made it illegal for one to live in or own property in the other's area. European areas were further split between whites, coloureds and Asians and the Property Owners' (Residential Property) Bill of 1970 allowed white inhabitants to petition the Minister to remove other races from their area. A 'denominational tribunal' was set up to determine the race of those concerned, families were thrown out of their homes and were even split in certain cases, with some children classified as white and others as coloured. African education budgets were slashed, primary schooling cut from eight to seven years and several multi-racial institutions were closed. Those that survived were under constant pressure.

Guerrilla activity began by the end of 1967 but had little effect at first. The Organisation for African Unity set up a clearing house in Dar es Salaam through which volunteers were sent to Moscow, Peking, Pyongkyang, Cuba, West Africa and Algeria for training. Arms were sent in from all round the world, although most came from China. The first two major infiltrations, in 1968, ended with over two-thirds of the nationalist forces dead and the rest scattered. South African police were drafted in to help the Rhodesian army.

First Attempts at Settlement

By now Britain had a Conservative Government willing to make greater concessions and in November 1971 a draft agreement was initialled making UDI legal and allowing the Rhodesian Front to remain in power, still using a split franchise. A new Declaration of Rights would not affect existing legislation and could be overridden by a State of Emergency—by now an almost permanent part of the political scene. Abel Muzorewa, Bishop of the Methodist Church in Rhodesia, now entered the arena, forming the African National Council, initially a peaceful body set up to explain the implications of the proposals to the people before the arrival of the Pearce Commission, a British survey
of public reaction, in January 1972. It was the first time that anyone had ever asked the Africans for their opinion and an overwhelming majority said no. The agreement foundered but the government had been forced to allow 'normal political activity' during the Commission's visit, and its chief result was a massive increase in support for the nationalist movements after a short but effective propaganda campaign.

This freedom didn't last long. By the end of 1972 the state of emergency had been renewed and political gatherings were banned in black areas. In 1973 national service was put up to a year, whole villages were being fined if suspected of harbouring terrorists, with no right of appeal to the courts, and the

89

ZANLA guerillas celebrating a victory

first executions for terrorist offences had taken place. The Zambian border was closed. A series of closed territories was created where police had the power to confiscate or destroy anything of use to the guerrillas and Africans thought to be in danger of being exposed to intimidation (i.e. any contact with guerrilla forces) were forcibly removed to 'protected villages'. By September the death penalty for harbouring terrorists was introduced and the villagers found themselves trapped, threatened by the guerrilla forces if they didn't cooperate and by the army if they did, while both sides became increasingly barbaric in their methods.

Barbarism on all sides

From about 1974 onwards events outside the country began to play an increasingly important role. Mozambique and Angola both went independent with strongly Marxist governments; Russia and China were pouring in more and more arms and finance; and Mozambique offered space and support for training camps, effectively opening up a second front. Other African leaders such as Kaunda in Zambia and Vorster in South Africa began to look for a settlement. And with more Communist involvement came American interest. Even Smith began to realise he was in a 'no win' situation, although he continued to swear that there would be 'no majority rule within a thousand years', and began a series of secret talks with Abel Muzorewa. Agreement was reached but overwhelmingly rejected when Muzorewa took it back to the African National Congress.

No win situation

Internal squabbling and tribal divisions started to hamper the nationalists. ZAPU was primarily Ndebele and was reluctant to send troops belonging to ZIPRA, its military branch, to Mozambique or into the east of Rhodesia while ZANU and its military wing ZANLA took full advantage of the support given by Mozambique's Samora Machel and Tanzania's Julius Nyerere. Only the prospect of major settlement talks forced the different groups to try and work together. On 8 December 1974 Nkomo, Sithole, Chikerema and Muzorewa signed a Declaration of Unity in Lusaka, refurbishing the Africa National Congress with Muzorewa as chairman. On 11 December the political detainees were released and a ceasefire announced to allow a new conference to go ahead without bias or preconditions. Discussions soon broke down and the ceasefire lasted only 24 hours.

Divisions amongst the nationalists

The gap between Nkomo and Sithole widened, ZANU split internally and the newly released Robert Mugabe took over most of the organisation, including the military. Muzorewa and Nkomo also quarrelled and Nkomo was expelled from the African National Congress. After further deadlocked talks in mid-1975 Muzorewa decided not to risk returning to Rhodesia and set up a Zimbabwe Liberation Committee in Lusaka as the external wing of the ANC, headed by Sithole. In September Nkomo called a meeting of the ANC in Salisbury and had himself elected president of the 'internal ANC', in reality ZAPU under another name, but while he still commanded the support of ZAPU even he had little power in Mashonaland. Nevertheless, he continued to talk to Smith.

Robert Mugabe   Mugabe, a shadowy and terrifying figure to the white Rhodesians, was rapidly becoming the one person of real importance in the nationalist ranks. He came from humble origins, a member of a minor Shona tribe, the Zezeru, on the eastern border. Educated at mission schools, he had been a teacher before his detention in Gwelo for ten years from 1964 where he spent his time studying and teaching, gaining several degrees along the way. In spite of his lack of hard experience, he was so well respected that by 1970 those ZANU leaders detained with him elected him as head of the organisation in place of Sithole. When in March 1975 Sithole was again detained, Mugabe escaped to Mozambique and set up ZANU headquarters in Quelimane, completely reorganising the rapidly growing party.

In January 1976 ZANLA and ZIPRA forces were merged, on paper at least, into ZIPA—the Zimbabwe People's Army. Shortly afterwards 1000 guerrillas crossed the border into northeast Rhodesia. In March Mozambique closed its border; in May national service was lengthened to 18 months; and in June the Rhodesian army began a series of brutal raids across the Mozambique border.

Henry Kissinger now went on a whirlwind tour of African capitals, gathering support for yet another conference. This time Smith agreed in advance to a package which would include an interim government with white control of law and order, an end to the war and sanctions, and majority rule within two years. Nkomo and Mugabe were persuaded to forget their differences and formed the Patriotic Front in October, but Mugabe then made a series of statements almost guaranteed to stop the conference before it began, claiming Marxist-Leninist principles, promising to nationalise all white land and put anyone connected with the Rhodesian government on trial. The conference still opened, but without hope of success.

Zimbabwe-Rhodesia

Ian Smith looked instead to the moderate black organisations, preparing the way with a series of acts designed to remove many forms of segregation. In 1977 nearly half the European land was opened to people of any race, and by the end of the year only health and education facilities remained barred to Africans. Smith then summoned Muzorewa, Sithole and Chief Jeremiah Chirau to secret talks, finally giving in to the principle of one man, one vote and agreeing a new constitution. This created a legislative assembly of 100 members, 72 black, elected by universal suffrage, and 28 white, their seats reserved for ten years, to be elected by a separate voters' roll and indirect elections. An executive council of presidential status would consist of the leader of the main white party (i.e. Smith himself) and the three black leaders. The cabinet would have an equal number of black and white ministers, paired to run the different portfolios. There was to be a justiciable Bill of Rights.

Too little too late This was accepted by many and the Zambian border reopened in October 1978, but by the time Smith stepped down and Muzorewa became first Prime Minister of the new state of Zimbabwe-Rhodesia on 1 May 1979, ZANU was claiming control of some 90 percent of the country and was establishing alternative governments at village and district level. The Patriotic Front overwhelmingly opposed the new regime and vowed to continue the fight. Muzorewa's appeal to the guerrillas to lay down their weapons led, if anything, to increased enrolment.

Reaction around the world was little better. In January 1978 British representatives met with PF leaders and promised not to make any settlement without them. When Smith claimed that he had now fulfilled the principles laid down by the *Tiger* talks and demanded that sanctions be lifted and

Nkomo and Mugabe studying the small print during the Lancaster House conference

that Zimbabwe-Rhodesia be given aid to fight against Communism, he was ignored.

War devastation The war was beginning to cripple the country. Over 10,000 had died already and over the next 18 months the death toll rose until nearly 1000 were dying every month. Over half a million villagers were living shanty existences on the outskirts of Salisbury and Bulawayo, or in refugee camps across the borders. 70 percent of white farms on the eastern border had been abandoned and over 10 million acres (4 million hectares) of farmland was vacant or underused. 500 schools, 17 hospitals and 52 clinics had closed. Some 10,000 guerrilla troops were operating inside Rhodesia, while there were about 20,000 more waiting across the borders. This number doubled by the end of 1979. In October 1978 all Africans between the ages of 18 and 25 were told to register for call-up. Many crossed the border instead.

Independence

In Britain the Conservatives won the 1979 election and were eager to reach a settlement. The new constitution was to be drawn up under British auspices with all parties involved in the negotiations and to be implemented after free and fair elections run by the British and monitored by the Commonwealth. The conference began on 10 September 1979 at Lancaster House, London, chaired by Lord Carrington, the British Foreign Secretary, who also led the British delegation.

London peace conference

Discussions dragged on for months as the Patriotic Front tried to abolish the white protected seats and install a presidential system of government. Mugabe stalled at every stage, hoping for a military breakthrough that would give him outright control. But when the talks threatened to drag on into the new year, Carrington lifted sanctions, sent Lord Soames out to Salisbury as governor and threatened to exclude the PF from the final agreement. This was eventually signed on 21 December 1979.

Transition to independence

Lord Soames was to have sole control over the transition period. A ceasefire was declared as of 28–29 December and all guerrilla forces had to report to designated assembly points within seven days.

The Southern Rhodesia Act, passed on 14 November, empowered Britain to govern directly, draw up a new constitution and call elections. On 12 December Lord Soames arrived in Salisbury and the country became legal again. On 20 December the Zimbabwe Bill was passed, allowing the country to become an independent republic outside the Commonwealth. Amnesty was granted for all political acts during the UDI period and a Commonwealth Monitoring Force of 1300 arrived to take control.

Ten parties registered for the elections which were held in February, Nkomo using the name Patriotic Front while Mugabe settled for ZANU (PF). Sithole used ZANU, and Muzorewa the now enfeebled African National Congress. With 500 British policemen and 80 British election supervisors in control and 291 other official observers from around the world, 94 percent of the electorate voted, and the elections were pronounced free and fair by almost all. It was an overwhelming victory for Mugabe, with ZANU (PF) taking 57 seats while Nkomo got 20 and Muzorewa only three.

Birth of modern Zimbabwe On 16 April 1980 the Reverend Canaan Banana, former chairman of the Bulawayo Council of Churches and vice-president of the ANC, was sworn into office as first president of an independent Zimbabwe at the Rufaso Football Stadium, Salisbury, in the presence of HRH Prince Charles. At midnight, the Union Jack was lowered and the new flag raised. Zimbabwe was born.

ZIMBABWE TODAY BACKGROUND

Today ZANU (PF) are still firmly in control of the country and are likely to remain so. The first few years of independence were troubled, and the government led a couple of major offensives against the mainly Ndebele ZAPU, one at least ending in a bloody massacre. A Unity Pact, signed by Mugabe and Nkomo, finally brought the bloodshed to an uneasy end in 1986, when Nkomo was brought back into the Cabinet as Senior Minister. ZANU and ZAPU officially merged into one party in November 1989, leaving the government with no effective opposition.

Edgar Tekere, formerly one of Mugabe's ministers, started a breakaway party, ZUM, in 1988, and gained a significant degree of support, particularly amongst the intelligentsia. For a variety of reasons, however, the party won virtually no seats in the latest elections, held in March 1990, when ZANU(PF) won another landside victory.

Government

Central government Parliament consists of two houses, a Senate and a House of Assembly. There are 40 senators, chosen by a combination of electoral colleges, the Council of Chiefs and Presidential nomination. The Assembly is made up of 100 members. Until 1987, 20 were protected white seats, when they became, effectively, presidential appointments. At the same time, many people from the main opposition parties joined ZANU (PF). The constitution set up by the Lancaster House Agreement was altered to create a presidential form of government, with Mugabe becoming President at the beginning of 1988. In April 1990, the 10 year period following the Lancaster House Agreement came to an end, leaving the government free to make any alterations they choose. Plans are underway to merge the two houses of parliament into a single house of 150 members, of whom 30 will be Presidential appointments. The country is still officially a multi-party state, and, although a great many statements are made to the contrary, seems likely to remain so.

Local government

At the local level the administration has been completely reformed along democratic socialist lines. Each village or group of villages of about 1000 people has a village development committee of four elected members and representatives of the youth and women's organisations. This is responsible for planning and carrying out small-scale projects, from co-operative farming or crafts projects to adult literacy programmes, from basic health care and family planning to pre-school education or providing shops. The village committees report to a Ward Development Committee, each ward having a population of about 6000. This in turn reports to a Rural District Council. The highest level of local government is the Provincial Council. There are eight provinces: Manicaland, Midlands, Matabeleland North, Matabeleland South, Masvingo and Mashonaland East, Central and West.

The position of white Zimbabweans

Although the government is theoretically on the hard left, in practice it has a healthy regard for private enterprise and has been soft-pedalling both on the introduction of a socialist economic structure and on its Africanisation programme to ensure that much-needed skills are not lost in a mass white exodus. Although most positions of power within the civil service and in many industries have now been given to blacks, more often than not their former white incumbents are still working alongside the new appointees. It will be years before there is a sufficient pool of black workers with enough hands-on experience to run the country unaided. Until then white expertise remains a valuable commodity and is carefully nurtured. Some of the whites grumble terribly about the appalling state the country is now in and how difficult it is to survive, but in reality they have experienced little or no drop in their exceptionally high standard of living. Most of them adapted within a few months and after their initial fear of Mugabe have now taken to terming him affectionately as 'Uncle Bob'. Some of those who left just before or after independence have returned to the country, and a number of newcomers are also going in, although generally only on short-term contracts.

Improving the lot of black farmers

At the lower end of the scale, many villages have been relocated to more fertile land and the old, desolate Tribal Trust Lands have been returned to the wild to give the vegetation a chance to recover. I have driven along stretches of road that I remembered as being near desert-like expanses of bare, eroded sand, now seeing instead mile upon mile of lush, verdant bush. Those white farms that had been abandoned or were being poorly run have been taken over and handed over to black farmers, most being carved up into small plots. The government does exercise a great deal of control over both agriculture and industry, but the profit motive is alive and kicking and never a day does past without some minister exhorting people to work harder and make more money, not to go straight into state pockets, but to increase the melting pot of the consumer economy.

Repairing the damage of war

Both government funds and the massive amounts of foreign aid that have poured into the country have been concentrated on repairing the damage done by the war and the recent disastrous droughts, reopening schools and cattle dips, building and repairing roads, overhauling the education system and trying to rebuild the country's food reserves. Education is now free and compulsory for all, although the vast influx of new children has put a severe strain on resources and there is still a serious shortage of books and teachers. Skilled expatriates and aid workers have been brought in to fill the gaps in local knowledge and run intensive training schemes as well as to work on a wide variety of projects from basic village health to agricultural research.

Zimbabwe's strengths . . .

The country is desperately short of money and is certainly not a model of efficiency in all ways, but in the main its future looks bright. In spite of the devastating effect of the war, the infrastructure inherited was one of the strongest in Africa, the soil is some of the most fertile and the resources at Zimbabwe's disposal are great. The government has proved itself to be sensible, moving slowly towards reform without frightening off investors. Nevertheless there are still some serious problems to be faced.

and its problems Zimbabwe has one of the highest birthrates in the world, and with a relatively well developed health service and low infant mortality rate the population is threatening to run out of control. Two of the biggest of the many social education programmes begun since independence are in women's rights and family planning, both of which are enthusiastically supported by the government and women, though at the moment only reluctantly by men. So far, neither has had a noticeable effect. If the birthrate cannot be reduced, the population explosion will wipe out any chance for the country's success. Caused partly by the population explosion, but also, ironically, by progress, there is also rampant unemployment. As more and more people get some education, they are leaving the land and flocking to the cities in search of skilled or white-collar jobs, which do not exist. With present levels of investment in industry, they are likely to do so in the foreseeable future.

In addition, there is the severe political strain of relations with neighbouring South Africa. Landlocked Zimbabwe is still heavily dependent on South Africa both economically and for transport and this cannot be lessened until such time as Mozambique is permanently at peace and the port at Beira is usable and freely accessible, an event still in the distant future. There are currently some 15,000 Zimbabwean troops in Mozambique trying to keep open a 16-km corridor either side of the Beira railway and pipeline, but this is little more than a holding operation and the route to the coast remains extremely unreliable.

The Economy

Private
enterprise
success

Agriculture and forestry. Farming is one of Zimbabwe's major and most successful industries, employing 280,000 people on a wide variety of properties from subsistence level smallholdings to massive plantations.

The sector is entirely in private hands, though the government has taken an active role in improving techniques and training, providing financing, offering veterinary control, setting prices and controlling marketing to provide some stability.

The main crops are maize, wheat, cotton, tobacco and sugar, although oilseeds such as soya and groundnuts are increasing and tea, coffee and a wide variety of fruits and vegetables are also grown. The weather is generally mild, and with the aid of major irrigation projects more and more people are planting two crops a year. Of the domestic animals, by far the largest number are cattle, with a national herd of some five million. Pigs, poultry and tough goat-like sheep are also farmed in smaller numbers and there is increasing interest in game ranching, with eland already being herded and trials underway with other antelope. The country is almost entirely self-sufficient in basic foods and until the recent droughts was exporting substantial amounts of maize and beef.

Forestry also plays a large part in the country's economy, employing about 14,000 workers and based mainly on such indigenous hardwoods as mukwa, mahogany and teak. 70,000 tonnes are cut each year for railway sleepers, furniture and flooring from natural forests 824,000 hectares in size.

Threatened
forests

Hardwoods grow far faster in this type of hot climate than in Europe, but the timber industry and the fact that wood is still the main fuel for most of the population are rapidly reducing forest areas which urgently need replanting. A World Bank project aiming to do just that is currently underway, also providing the research and training necessary to extend forest areas and provide for more careful exploitation in the future. The country also has a growing number of softwood plantations of pine, wattle and eucalyptus in the Eastern Highlands.

Mining. Although the mines don't employ as many people as the farms, mining is probably still the country's most important industry, accounting for seven percent of gross national product and nearly 40 percent of valuable foreign exchange earnings. 40 minerals are mined in Zimbabwe, though 90 percent of output is from only seven of them: gold, asbestos, nickel, coal, copper, chromite and tin, and only the chromite and asbestos deposits are large by world standards.

Major foreign exchange earner

Manufacturing. For a small country the manufacturing base is surprisingly large, and while there is not a wide variety of goods there are few necessities that need to be imported. Heavy industry includes metal production and manufacture including making rolling stock and other heavy machinery. A growing chemical industry includes fertilisers, paint, pharmaceuticals and cosmetics. Lighter industries include food and drink, clothes and shoes, wood and furniture, as well as paper and print. By 1986, 6500 different products were being manufactured in Zimbabwe, accounting for about 25 percent of GNP and employing 16 percent of the country's workforce.

Power. Almost all the country's power still comes from the massive hydro-electric complex at Kariba, though there is now a small coal-fired thermal station at Hwange and plans are afoot for another massive hydro project on the Zambezi.

Water. As everywhere in Africa the country has been caught by recent serious droughts, which have devastated agriculture and led to a need for international food aid for the first time in Zimbabwe's history, in spite of wide networks of dams, lakes, rivers and bore-holes.

Tourism. Tourism took such a sharp dive it almost died before independence; only recently has Zimbabwe's image recovered sufficiently for tourists to start coming back. About 600,000 foreigners visited the country in 1991, the numbers slowly rising at about ten percent per annum. New hotels and resorts are opening, including the Sheraton in Harare, complete with a major conference facility.

Gradual recovery

The People and their Homes. The only detailed survey of Zimbabwe's population was done early in 1980, before the February elections. Since then tribal identity has offically been frowned upon except in a few small folk villages set up for tourists. Tribalism is meant to be a thing of the past, damaging to the stability of the fledgling state. In reality, of course, old traditions die hard.

There are 12 main groups in the country, 11 large tribes, all split into further sub-groups, and a white and Asian population of about 200,000. Overall, the population is about ten million.

The Shona

By far the largest proportion (77 percent) of this is made up of the Shona tribes, who live in the centre, north and east of the country.

The Shona are split into six main tribes, the Rozwi, Korekore, Zezeru, Manyika, Karanga and Ndau, but there are 65 linguistic sub-groupings. The Zezeru alone have eight while the Karanga have 15.

In the southeast are the Venda and the Shangaan, and a small area along the shores of Lake Kariba is Tonga territory.

The Ndebele

The rest of the country belongs to the Ndebele tribes, which include the Ndebele themselves and the related Kalanga, later converts to the Ndebele tradition. The Ndebele have 12 sub-groups.

Architecture in Zimbabwe isn't anything to write home about. There are a few colonial buildings left from before the First World War, with their wide verandahs and cool stone floors, but white ants are a real danger to buildings, particularly the early mud brick ones, and few have survived the ravages

Rural housing

Practical housing

of the ants. By Zimbabwean standards a house built in the 1950s is old. The homes of the more affluent are generally sprawling bungalows with bright red tiles or corrugated iron roofs and acres of window. The high density housing areas (the old townships) are usually full of small rectangular two-room houses all cheek by jowl and brightly coloured. In rural areas, most people still live in small villages, in round thatched mud huts surrounded by mealie patches and herds of goats. Yet even here there is a rapid change to longer-lasting rectangular huts built from brick or breeze-block.

SECTION 2:
MASHONALAND

Harare and Environs

Lake McIlwaine

Chinhoyi Caves

HARARE AND ENVIRONS

Getting There and Getting Around

Harare is the hub of Zimbabwe for the purposes of transport as in every other way, with international and domestic flights serving the airport, rail links to many internal destinations as well as to Botswana, Zambia, Mozambique and South Africa, and good roads to all major destinations and border crossings.

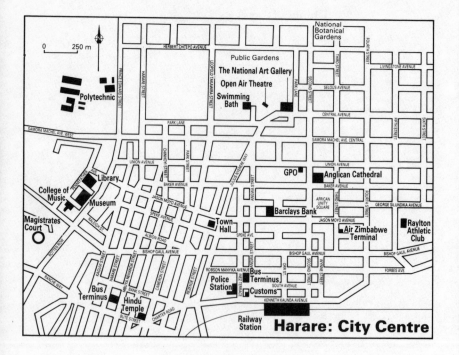

Harare: City Centre

Into and out of Harare   The **airport** is about 15 km from the centre of town, with regular cheap bus transfers to the Air Zimbabwe terminal at the corner of Third Street and Speke Avenue, opposite Meikles Hotel (just behind African Unity Square).

The **railway station** is on Kenneth Kaunda Avenue, within walking distance of the centre of town (Tel: 700011, or 700033 after hours).

There are plenty of taxis. The main **taxi rank** is on African Unity Square.

There are two important bus terminals.

The main bus terminal, both for **intercity and suburban buses**, is on Rezende Street, between Stanley Avenue and Baker Avenue, **Local suburban buses** are run by the Harare United Omnibus Company, Tel: 725670. Times and destinations are posted at the bus station. There are a number of **intercity bus companies** and all services are bookable.

Express Motorway: Tel: 720392.
American Express Travel Service: Tel: 703421.
Mitchell Cotts Travel: Tel: 703683.

All of these also have offices in other main centres or are bookable through travel agents.

Buses to outlying districts and rural areas run from the Mbare Bus Terminal, Chaminuke and Ardbennie Roads. There are no timetables, so just turn up and wait for the next one.

The **car hire firms** Avis, Hertz and Europcar are all represented in Zimbabwe, with their head offices in Harare. Hertz and Avis both have branches at the airport. All can be booked before you arrive and arrangements can be made for your car to meet you.

Getting around Harare The centre of the city is easily small enough to walk around, although the suburbs sprawl for miles. Taxis are cheap and as the city is very flat cycling is easy. For sightseeing in town and the surrounding areas, UTC runs a variety of tours; otherwise hire a car. Local buses are plentiful but schedules are unreliable.

History

On 11 September 1890 the pioneer column arrived on the Mashonaland plateau, reaching Mount Hampden. Major Frank Johnson, who led the column, climbed the Kopje and 'saw something that fascinated me more than Mount Hampden. It was

Harare panorama

The founding of Fort Salisbury

a beautiful open plain with rich, red soil, non-swampy and obviously ideal agricultural land ... bounded to the south by a stream, which would be ideal for a good-sized town'. He suggested this as the site for the new capital. Jameson agreed, and on 13 September the Union Jack was hoisted to a 21-gun salute and the settlement named Fort Salisbury after the British Prime Minister.

On the same day the column was disbanded and within three months the first fort and settlement had been built. Trouble started soon afterwards with the onset of the rains, which brought malaria and blackwater fever, and cut off the settlement from its supply route to the south, leaving the inhabitants to live on dry biscuits and what they could scratch from their surroundings for five months.

By the middle of the following year a few women and children began to arrive, and the first few permanent buildings—stores and hotels—were erected. The government surveyed the area and decided that the slightly higher ground away from the Kopje (modern Causeway) was a better site.

It tried to persuade people to move, but the shop-keepers demanded compensation so the government built its own offices here instead. Within a short while two distinct and feuding communities had grown up. When the railway arrived in 1899 the station had to be built exactly halfway between the two areas to avoid further bad feeling.

It was a touchy place at the best of times. After Lobengula's downfall many settlers were moving to Bulawayo, and Bulawayo got a railway line first. Salisbury's inhabitants demanded written reassurance from Rhodes that it would remain the capital. They got it, and it has remained capital ever since, the only place in the country where any real decisions are taken.

'The one who does not sleep' The largest of the black suburbs has always been known as Harare. In 1980 when the country gained its independence the name of the entire city was changed. Harare means 'the one who does not sleep' and was the name of an ancient chief in the area who gained a reputation for being particularly alert.

Harare Today

Today Harare has a population of around one million and an area of about 540 sq km, but even so the overwhelming impression is of a small, peaceful country town. The wealthier suburbs sprawl in a glow of large and richly coloured gardens; the poorer, high density areas are much more cluttered but still brightly coloured and without any of the frenetic quality you might expect in city life. The centre is small, with low, white, slightly shabby buildings and wide streets. It never seems to be crowded or hurried and you can almost always guarantee a parking place within a couple of minutes' walk of where you want to be.

Making preparations Even so, everything is organised from here, from the government through to travelling. If you want your journey around Zimbabwe to run smoothly, you will head straight for Harare and spend a couple of days sorting out itineraries and making bookings. If you don't, you will probably find yourself waiting anyway while every request is referred back to the capital.

The **Harare Publicity Association** is on the corner of Jason Moyo Avenue and Second Street (African Unity Square), PO Box 1483, Harare. Tel: 705085/6. It publishes a monthly newsletter with news of what is on and provides advice and information about accommodation, food, etc.

Accommodation

Harare is the only town in Zimbabwe with a wide range of accommodation spanning the full price range. The selection below singles out some of the better options in each bracket.

Upmarket hotels. With the possible exception of the Sheraton, none of these hotels is architecturally interesting, being of the concrete block school. All however are extremely comfortable with excellent service and a variety of good (if not astounding) food. Upwards of US$80 a night.

*Sheraton*****: The newest and most glamorous hotel in town. Slightly out of the centre on Pennefather Avenue, opposite the museum. Style and prices on the true international level. PO Box 3033, Harare. Tel: 729771. Fax: 728450. Reservations: Tel: 728728. Telex: 26574 SHEREX ZW.

*Meikles*****: One of the first hotels to be built in town, and though it moved some years ago into a more modern building it still prides itself on old-fashioned charms and service. Right in the centre, overlooking African Unity Square, PO Box 594, Harare. Tel: 795655. Fax: 707754.

*Monomotapa*****: Large and very comfortable, with probably the best views of the city from its top floors. On Julius Nyerere Ave, near the Art Gallery and Park. Tel: 704501. Fax: 791920 Bookings through Zimbabwe Sun Central Reservations Office: Tel: 736644.

*Jameson*****: Again very pleasant, noted for superb services. Corner of Samora Machel Avenue and

Park Street. Run by Cresta Hotels. PO Box 2833, Harare. Tel: 794641. Fax: 794655. Reservations: Tel: 703131.

Holiday Inn****: Similar to Holiday Inns the world over. Now run by Zimbabwe Sun. Corner of Samora Machel Avenue and Fifth Street. PO Box 7, Harare. Tel: 795611. Fax: 735695.

Mid-range hotels. These are all very comfortable, with full service, restaurants, bars, swimming pools, etc. Rates start at Z$70 to Z$80 a night.

Oasis***: Run by Cresta. 124 Baker Avenue (between Fifth and Sixth Streets). PO Box 1541, Harare. Tel: 704217. Telex: 22099 OASIS ZW.

Ambassador**: Run by the Zimbabwe Tourist Development Corporation. 88 Union Avenue. PO Box 872, Harare. Tel: 708121. Telex: 22654 AMB ZW.

Courteney**: A bit far from the centre to walk. Corner of Selous Avenue and Eighth Street. PO Box 3150. Tel: 706411/4.

Budget hotels. The following hotels are all registered with the tourist board but are ungraded. Prices are cheap but quality may be doubtful.

Bronte Hotel: 132 Baines Avenue. Tel: 796631.

Elizabeth Hotel: Corners of Julius Nyerere Way and Robert Mugabe Road. Tel: 708591.

International Hotel: Corner of Fourth Street and Baker Avenue. Tel: 700332.

Executive Hotel: Samora Machel Ave. Tel: 792803.

Federal Hotel: 9 Harare Street. Tel: 706118.

Queens Hotel: Corner of Robert Mugabe Road and Kaguvi Street. Tel: 738977.

The Elizabeth, International, Queens and Federal all belong to Central African Hotels and are clean and hygienic, if noisy. There are other registered cheap hotels, a list of which can be obtained from the tourist board, as well as some with no official standing.

Hostels. There is a *youth hostel* at the western end of Josiah Chinamano Avenue, some way from the city centre. Tel: 796436. It is affiliated to but not a full member of the YHA and standards leave something to be desired. The *Toc-H Hostel* (for men only) is a little better, also out of town, at the eastern end of Baines Avenue.

Camping. Always the best bet in this country if you are on a low budget.
Coronation Park: The municipal camping and caravan site is 6 km from the city centre off the Mutare Road. Space for 100 tents or caravans, with full, good facilities and attractive gardens. PO Box 1583, Harare. Tel: 46282.

Things to See in Harare
Parliament Building, corner of Baker Avenue and Third Street. Originally built as a hotel in 1895, the Parliament moved in in 1899 and has been there ever since. A new facade was added in 1938 and an extension was built in 1953 to house the Federal Assembly. Plans for a new parliamentary building, to be sited on the Kopje, are still on the drawing board. Guided tours can be arranged any weekday when Parliament is not sitting, or Mondays and Fridays when it is. There is a Visitors' Gallery in the main assembly room with spaces bookable in advance. If you arrive without notice, you may be able to visit the Strangers' Gallery. Dress should be smart or you will not be allowed in. Phone or write to the Chief Information Officer, Parliament of Zimbabwe, PO Box 8055, Causeway, Harare. Tel: 700181.

Colonial architecture There are few historic buildings of any real note, though there are still some nice examples of the colonial style with wrought iron and long verandahs dotted amongst the more modern blocks. Cecil House, Town House, Old Market Hall and Jameson House are worth looking at.

Cecil House, Built in 1901, it has been carefully restored and extended in the same style by the Mining Industry Pension Fund.

Town House, on Julius Nyerere Way. Built in 1932 in a neo-renaissance style around a central courtyard, it now houses the Mayor's Parlour and Town Clerk's Dept. The floral clock facing the front steps was installed in 1950 to commemmorate the town's Diamond Jubilee.

Old Market Hall, in Market Square, corner of Mbuya Nehanda Street and Bank Street. Built in 1894 and recently renovated.

Rural craft market **Jameson House**, Samora Machel Avenue. Originally built in 1896 as the High Court of Mashonaland, it now houses The Market, a government-run shop selling crafts from rural areas.

Anglican Cathedral, at the corner of Baker Avenue and Second Street. A remarkably ugly neo-something building started in 1913 and finished in 1961, erected on the site of the first pioneer church in the settlement. All that remains of this is an altar cross made of cigar boxes, now housed in the St George Chapel.

Queen Victoria Museum, Pennefather Avenue, opposite the Harare Sheraton. Part of the Civic Centre complex that also include the Magistrates' Court, municipal offices, City Library, National Sports Centre and Courtauld Concert Hall. Small and rather moth-eaten now, but still interesting, with good displays of local fauna. Open from 9am to 5pm seven days a week.

National Gallery, corner of Julius Nyerere Ave) and Park Lane. A small but attractive gallery founded in 1957 with a permanent exhibition including some lesser-known European artists and an excellent display of Shona sculpture. It is also home to touring exhibitions, special displays, lectures, workshops and films. Well worth a visit. Open 9am to 5pm Tuesday to Sunday. Closed Mondays. PO Box 8155, Causeway, Harare. Tel: 704666.

National Archives, out of the town centre, too far to walk, on the Borrowdale Road. Founded in 1935, the collection includes a broad photographic study of the country's past as well as written material. Open to the public for tours or research, Monday to Friday 7.45am to 4.30pm, Saturday 8am to noon. Closed Sundays and Bank Holidays.

Tobacco Auction Rooms. Auctions are held every morning during the selling season (roughly late April through September). Zimbabwe is one of the world's leading tobacco growers and this is one of the largest floors in the world. Absolutely fascinating: visitors are welcome and guided tours are possible. The first cigarettes were being made in Salisbury by 1894, and by 1913 tobacco was being exported. By 1930 it had become the mainstay of the Rhodesian economy, a position it has held ever since. The first auction was held in April 1936; in 1964 the Harare auction rooms became the first in the world to sell over 45 million kilos of flue-cured tobacco in one season. The sales start at 7.45am and some 6000 bales are sold by noon each day, with the farmer able to pick up his cheque in the afteroon. Check with the Publicity Association in African Unity Square (Tel: 705085/6) or the Tobacco Marketing Board's information department (Tel: 66311) for details.

World-class tobacco dealings

Harare Gardens, main public park, between Park Lane and Leopold Takawira Street. Very lush, green and shady, beautifully kept, with fountains, children's playground, open-air theatre, restaurant, and art displays and concerts over the weekends. The main public swimming pool (Olympic-size) is next door.

African Unity Square (formerly Cecil Square) is a much smaller park, also very pretty, originally established as a memorial to the pioneers. There is a flower market along the Jason Moyo Avenue side of the square. This is where the flag was first raised over the newly founded city, and the square is still considered the central landmark.

The Kopje is outside the city centre to the south-west, reached from either Rotten Row or Robert Mugabe Road. This is about the only hill in the area, with panoramic views over the city and the surrounding countryside and a toposcope laid out to show the direction and distance of the various points of interest. It was originally made into a memorial to the pioneers at the beginning of the century but now houses the Eternal Flame of Independence, lit on 18 April 1980 to mark the creation of independent Zimbabwe. The hill is the projected site of the new Parliament Building.

Panoramic views

Mbare Market—both Mbare (originally called Harare, until the whole city took the name) and Highfields, the two largest of the high density suburbs are fascinating and well worth a visit. The market in Mbare is a must, however, one of the largest I've seen, selling everything from deep fried worms to tractor tyres. Open every day until around 5.30pm, just behind the main Mbare bus station.

Restaurants
L'Escargot, Courteney Hotel, Tel: 706411. One of the best in town. Sort of French and expensive by Harare standards. Usually necessary to book.
Sandro's, 50 Union Ave/Julius Nyerere Way. Tel: 792460. Vaguely Italian with steak. Music in the evenings.
Guido's, Montague Shopping Centre, Josiah Chimano Ave. Tel: 723349. Cheap, cheerful and very popular, so you might have to queue, but worth it.
DV8, Groombridge Shopping Centre, The Chase, Groombridge. Tel: 39798.
Le Français, 7 Arts Complex, Avondale, Harare. Tel: 307706.
The National Handicraft Centre, Cnr Grant St/Chinhoyi St. Tel: 721816. Pan-African restaurant.

Surrounding Area
Chapungu Kraal, 8 km from the centre of Harare on the Doon Estate (off the Mutare Road). There

Shona life and culture

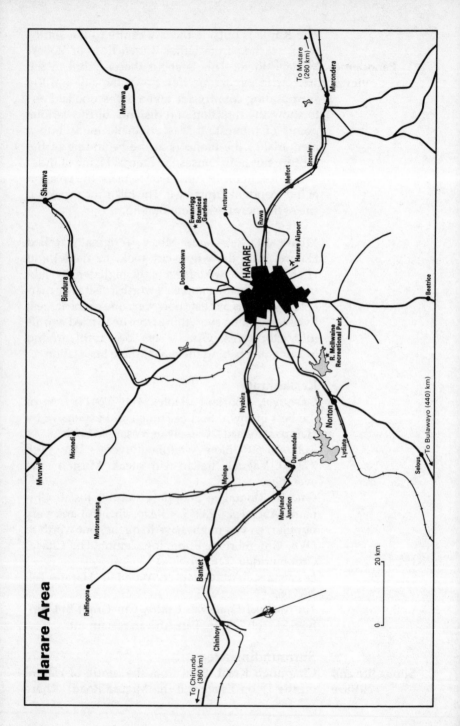

Harare Area

To Mutare (260 km)

Marondera

Murewa

Bromley

Meffort

Shamva

Arcturus

Ruwa

Ewanrigg Botanical Gardens

Dombashawa

HARARE

Harare Airport

Bindura

Beatrice

R. Mcilwaine Recreational Park

Nyabira

Norton

To Bulawayo (440) km)

Mvurwi

Msonedi

Darwendale

Lydiate

Selous

Mpinga

Motorashanga

Maryland Junction

Banket

Raffingora

20 km

Chinhoyi

0

To Chirundu (360 km)

is a traditionally built Shona village (thatched huts) to look around, a n'ganga (witchdoctor) to consult about your fortune and a permanent display of over 350 pieces of Shona sculpture. On Saturday at 3pm and Sunday at 11am and 3pm are displays of tribal music and dance. Open seven days a week. Doon Estate, 1 Harrow Road, Beverley East, Msasa. PO Box 1873, Harare. Tel: 47472/47533. Telex: 4559 VERDAF.

Epworth Balancing Rocks, on the land of the Epworth Mission, about 12 km from Harare on the Chiremba Road. The whole area surrounding Harare is littered with fascinating surreal rock formations created by centuries of erosion. These are the most spectacular of all and are the ones used on Zimbabwean bank notes.

Ewanrigg Botanical Gardens, 41 km from Harare on the Shamva Road. Run by the National Parks Service, the landscaped gardens cover 40 hectares and there are a further 200 hectares of untouched bush with paths laid out for walking. Especially renowned for their collections of aloes and cycads, the gardens are superbly run to show the indigenous flora off to best advantage as well as including a wide variety of species from other parts of the world. There are also water gardens and a large selection of cacti and herbs. All species are labelled with common, botanical and sometimes Shona names. Open from 8am every day. PO Box 8115, Causeway, Harare. Tel: Arcturus (174) 23720.

Heroes Acre, the National Memorial to the dead of the War of Liberation, 5 km from the city centre on the Bulawayo Road. Built by the Koreans at a cost of millions, it is a classic example of that vast, forbidding, monumental style of 'warheroes' art that is guaranteed to strike awe, if not fear, into the heart of any capitalist Westerner. Visits by appointment only on weekdays. Contact the Public Relations Office, Ministry of Information,

PO Box 8150, Causeway, Harare. Tel: 706891. Or call at Room 513, Fifth Floor, Liquenda House, Baker Avenue, Harare.

A close look at birds ...

Larvon Bird Gardens, 17 km from Harare off the Bulawayo Road, on Oatlands Road. Over 400 species of birds from all over the world (though the majority are natives to Zimbabwe), in pleasant surroundings that provide a rare opportunity to study them at close quarters. Open from 11am to 5pm weekdays (except Thursdays) and 9am to 5pm on weekends and public holidays. PO Box 8312, Causeway, Harare. Tel: 277496.

and lions

Lion Park, at the Le Rhone Game Farm, about 24 km from Harare on the Bulawayo Road. Originally founded to provide animals for films, there is a greater concentration of animals here than you are likely to find in the bush. Not exactly authentic, but if you want to guarantee getting close to lions, this is your chance. Open daily from 8.30am to 5pm. PO Box 733, Harare. Tel: Norton (172) 6437/9.

Mukuvisi Woodlands, 7 km from the city centre on the Mutare Road and Glenara Avenue (near the campsite), is a 265-hectare area of natural woodland with walks and picnic areas. 109 hectares has been reserved as a wildlife area. Walking safaris are conducted on the second, third and fourth weekends of every month. Phone 34715 or 36502 after 6pm for details.

Rock paintings, at Domboshawa. 25 km from the city on the Borrowdale Road. A steep climb. And at the Markwe Caves near the Imire private game park, 105 km from Harare off the Mutare Road. Contact Imire Game Park, Post Bag 3750, Marondera. Tel: Wedza 5040/5032/5042.

LAKE McILWAINE

The Hunyani River was dammed in 1952 to create a reservoir to act as Harare's main water supply. The resulting lake, 16 km long and covering an area of 57 sq km, was named after Sir Robert McIlwaine, the first chairman of the National Resources Board. This has now become Harare's main playground with a wide variety of entertainments as well as a small game reserve. The whole area of 5,550 hectares, 32 km west of Harare, has been designated a national park.

Getting There

Take the Bulawayo Road out of town. There are three signed turn-offs from it to the lake. The first, about 16 km from the city, leads to a tea garden, swimming pool, yacht club, the angling societies, the ranger's office and caravan club; the next, 29 km from Harare (turn by the Shell garage), goes to a hotel, tea garden, boating station, caravan and camping site, rowing club and picnic area; the third, 32 km from the city (by the Hunyani River Bridge), leads to the south bank of the lake, the warden's office, the dam wall and spillway. A further turn-off from this road just before reaching the wall leads to the National Parks rest camp.

What to Do at the Lake

Pony safaris

There are numerous opportunities for walking, fishing, watersports and game viewing. You can be guided along pony trails through the game park twice a day. Enquire at the Tourist Reception Office. The game park is about 1600 hectares in size and includes a wide variety of antelope and larger animals such as rhino, many of which have been introduced from other reserves. There is an exceptionally wide variety of birds in the area.

Accommodation

There is one **hotel**, the *Hunyani Hills***: Small (13 rooms) with mid-range prices. It has its own swimming pools, gardens and jetty, and can arrange for watersports and fishing. PO Box 2852, Harare. Tel: Norton (172) 236.

Situated within the game park on the south bank, there is a selection of two-bedroomed **lodges**, and **chalets** with one, two or three bedrooms. They are well equipped, but you must take in all your own food as there is no restaurant and no food shop. Post Bag 962, Norton. Tel: (172) 229. Bookings through National Parks Central Booking Office, Harare. The nearest supplier of food and fuel is the Turn Pike Garage, 16 km away.

There are three **campsites** and **caravan sites** in the area. The National Parks Service runs a *caravan site next to the Hunyani Hills Hotel*, and the *Msasa Camp Site* near the Jacana Yacht Club. Both are on the north bank and have full facilities. There are no camping sites within the game park. Book through the National Parks Central Bookings Office, Harare. *Admiral's Cabin* is a privately run camping and caravan site on the north bank with restaurant, swimming pool, caravans for hire and fishing and water sports facilities. PO Box 139, Norton. Tel: (172) 2642673.

CHINHOYI CAVES

The caves are 10 km north-west of Chinhoyi town which is 122 km from Harare on the main Harare-Chirundu road. Formerly known as the Sinoia Caves, their present name is from the Mashona Chief Chinhoyi who controlled the area when Selous, the first white man to see the caves, arrived in 1887. Chinhoyi had fenced off the entrance, created food stores underground and used the caves as a retreat to escape from Matabele raiding parties. The caves have long been used by humans, the earliest remains yet discovered giving a radio-carbon date of around AD 650.

The Largest Cave

Originally thought to be an ancient mine working, the largest cave is actually a massive sinkhole created when a circular area of the ground surface collapsed into a limestone cavern beneath. Looking down from the rim you can see a deep pool 46 metres below. This, known as the **Sleeping Pool**, is up to 91 metres deep and a dark crystal-clear blue in which it is easily possible to see rock formations and fish many metres below the surface. The Shona name for the pool is Chirorodziva, or 'the pool of the fallen', from an episode in the 1830s when the Angoni tribe surprised the locals and threw them into it. The pool remains at a constant temperature of 22°C throughout the year. There are several underwater passages leading from the pool, not all of which have been explored, and it is thought that this collapsed cave is only part of a much larger system including bigger bodies of water.

'The pool of the fallen'

There are two paths leading down to the edge of the Sleeping Pool, one through the main entrance and down a sloping passage, the other through the Dark Cave to a point just above the water on the far side of the pool. This has some

Descending to the pool

very steep stairs and narrow passages and isn't recommended unless you are reasonably fit.

The caves are a National Park. PO Box 193, Chinhoyi. Tel: Chinhoyi 2550.

Hotels and Camping

Caves Motel*: Small and simple, mid-range prices, right next to the caves. PO Box 230, Chinhoyi. Tel: 2340.

Orange Grove Motel**: Larger and with more facilities such as a restaurant and swimming pool. Also mid-range prices. In Chinhoyi town. Independence Way, PO Box 436, Chinhoyi. Tel: 2785/6.

The National Parks Service runs a *camping and caravan site* next to the caves. Booking is not necessary.

SECTION 3:
ALONG THE ZAMBEZI

Mana Pools

Kariba

Lake Kariba

Victoria Falls

Hwange National Park

THE ZAMBEZI AND MANA POOLS

The Zambezi

The Zambezi, 2700 km long, is Africa's fourth longest river. It has probably one of the most evocative names in the history of exploration and adventure, conjuring images of hair-raising rapids, crocodiles and Victorian gentlemen in topis.

The course of the Zambezi

It rises in northern Zambia, near Kalene Hill, and flows southwest into Angola before turning back into Zambia. From there it goes south across the Barotse Plain and into the Caprivi swamps where it is joined by the Chobe. Then it turns east to form the border between Zambia and Zimbabwe, finally flowing across northern Mozambique and out into the Indian Ocean.

The main Zambezi River used to flow south from Caprivi to join the Limpopo (which forms the southern boundary between South Africa and Zimbabwe). The north-flowing Matetsi River was the source of the Lower Zambezi, and the stretch which now runs between the confluences of the Chobe and the Matetsi did not exist at all.

During the volcanic upheavals of the Jurassic period (about 150 million years ago), the old river was split in two. The Limpopo continued to flow into the Indian Ocean, but the northern section was cut off from the coast and began to form a huge inland swamp of which only the Makarika Salt Pan, the Okavango and the Chobe Swamps now remain. As its level rose it began to spill over a low-lying area to the east to join the course of the old Matetsi River. This is the river's present course.

The river's gift to southern Africa

As well as being one of the world's best natural boundaries, the Zambezi now fuels two of the world's largest hydro-electric projects, at Kariba on the Zambia–Zimbabwe border, and Caborabasa in Mozambique, while a third is under discussion. It is also the heart of Zimbabwe's tourist trade, with sights like Victoria Falls and the great lake at Kariba, activities such as superb white-water rafting, canoeing and fishing, and along its banks some of the wildest and most game-rich country in southern Africa.

Mana Pools

Over the years part of the Zambezi has slowly moved north, leaving behind it on the south bank the vast series of terraces, small streams and pools known as Mana Pools, 300 km north of Harare. An area of about 2500 sq km has now been turned into **Remote and** a national park, one of the most remote, most beau-**beautiful** tiful and best stocked in Africa.

Because of its remoteness and the poor state of some of its roads the park is open only between the beginning of May and the end of October. You should always check on the condition of the roads before you go in and take plenty of fuel, food and water with you.

Getting There

By road. Take the main road north to Makuti, which is the turn-off point and also the last place you will be able to get oil or petrol. 16 km further on you will reach Marongora where you must get an entry permit before going any further. You must leave here by 3.30pm at the latest to make it to the park camps before they close for the night. 6 km beyond Marongora a gravel road turns to the right. Follow this for 30 km to reach Nyakasikana Gate and the entrance to the park. The park office at Nyamepi Camp is 42 km further on. The entry fee is payable here. Only 50 vehicles are allowed into the park at any one time, vehicles weighing over 3 tonnes or carrying more than 20 people are prohibited, and every camp pitch is limited to only one vehicle, so check before leaving to make sure you will be allowed in.

By boat. Entry by boat is forbidden. Canoe trips along the Lower Zambezi between Kariba and Kanyemba are allowed only with a permit obtain able from the National Parks Head Office. 1, Josiah Tongogara Ave/Colquoun St, Box 8365, Causeway, Harare. Tel: 707624.

By air. The privately owned safari camps on the edge of the park run small planes from Kariba for their guests. Otherwise you can hire a plane to take you in—if you can afford it. Ask at Kariba airport.

Accommodation
The **National Parks Office** runs two **lodges** and four **campsites** within the park boundary.

Nyamepi Camp has 40 camping or caravan sites with full facilities. *Nkupe Camp*, 1 km to the east, *Mucheni Camp*, 8 km to the west, and *Vundu Camp*, 13 km upstream, are remote, very small campsites with no real facilities, limited to a maximum of 12 people and two vehicles. Vundu has some sleeping huts.

Musanga Lodge to the east of Nyamepi and *Muchichiri Lodge* to the west are self-contained and fully-equipped, sleeping between six and eight people.

These must all be booked well in advance through the National Parks Central Booking Office, PO Box 8151, Harare. Tel: 706077.

These are also two **privately run safari camps**.
Chikwenya Camp: Has a series of small sleeping huts but all other life is out of doors. All meals are provided as are safari tours by boat or road. Bookings to Chikwenya Safaris, Post Bag 2081, Kariba. Tel: Kariba 2253.
Ruckomechi Camp: Run by Mana Pools Safaris, takes a maximum of 16 people at any one time, living in thatched huts. It offers tours by boat, open Land Rover or canoe, as well as tours on foot and at night. Book through Garth Thompson Safari Consultants, Room 410/411 Monomotapa Hotel, PO Box 5826, Harare. Tel: Harare 7952/87. Telex: 2364 ZW. 2364 ZW

Things to Do
Game viewing. This lush area holds one of the greatest concentrations of wildlife in Zimbabwe,

Lake Kariba and Mana Pools National Park

To Lusaka (125 km)

River Zambezi

ZAMBIA

Rucomechi Camp

Chikwenya Camp

Kanyemba

R. Rucomechi

R. Chewore

Chirundu

Makuti

Mana Pools National Park

Kariba

Fothargill Island

Karoi

Bumi Hills

Matusadona National Park

Lake Kariba

ZIMBABWE

To Harare (292 km)

Binga

Chizarira National Park

0   50 km

Large herds of elephants and buffalos including herds of 12,000 elephants and 16,000 buffalos. It is one of the few places where you are allowed out of your car unsupervised, though you are strongly advised to be extremely cautious.

Fishing. You are allowed to take up to six fish per person per day with no licence. Take your own equipment.

Canoeing. There are several companies, including those mentioned above under accommodation, that offer three- to four-day canoe trips along the Zambezi through the National Park area. Among them are:
Canoeing Safaris, PO Box 2625, Harare. Tel: 26513. Telex: 4187 ZW.
Mana Pools Safaris, 39 Lonsdale Road, Avondale, Harare. Tel: 83496.
Michael Gardner Associates, PO Box 825, Harare. Tel: 885127.

127

KARIBA

Getting Around

There is a good tarred road with a regular coach service from Harare. There are also daily flights from Harare to Kariba, met by a Buffalo Safaris bus. Transfers to the town or your hotel cost Z$15 each way. Hire a car if staying in the town as it is strung out over a long distance and there is only one taxi, which charges what it likes. The nearer lodges on the lake are reached by boat, those further away by private plane. You can also hire boats, either motor cruisers or yachts. A car ferry service operates along the length of Lake Kariba from Mbilizi to Kariba town, taking 22 hours each way. It leaves Kariba on Mondays, returning on Tuesdays, but only if there is sufficient demand. Details from Kariba Ferries, PO Box 278, Harare. Tel: Harare 65476 or Kariba 460.

The Kariba Dam

The local people, the Tonga, have a modern-day legend about Lake Kariba. The river god, Nyami Nyami, who has the head of a fish and the tail of a snake, had a wife who went down the Zambezi.

The wife who cannot come home

While she was gone the white men came and began building the wall. He tried every way he could to stop them but to no avail and it was completed. But one day Nyami Nyami will find a way of knocking it down so that his wife can come home.

If he did, the ensuing flood would destroy half of Zimbabwe and all of Mozambique.

The idea of damming Kariba Gorge was first suggested in 1912 to provide water for irrigation, and a survey was taken with this in mind in 1914. But nothing more was done until 1941 when the site was again proposed as one of four possible sites for a major hydro-electric scheme. It was 1951 before it was decided that the dam should be placed here. In 1956 contracts were signed, with Richard

Kariba Dam, linking Zimbabwe and Zambia

Costain to build the township, and with Impresit, an Italian consortium, to construct the dam.

Work started promptly with a series of six coffer dams and the excavation of a massive underground cavern (150 metres underground, 140 metres long, 40 metres high and 23 metres wide) to hold the power station. Several disasters struck along the way, including major floods that swept away the suspension bridge and main coffer dam. But by December 1958 the main wall was blocking the gorge, the river stopped flowing and the lake began to fill. In June 1959 the dam wall reached its full height. In December the first generator was commissioned and on 17 May 1960 the power station was officially opened by the Queen Mother.

The human and financial costs . . . The dam had taken 10,000 men four years to build at a cost of Z$180 million. 87 men lost their lives, including 18 who fell into the fresh concrete in

129

February 1959. 14 bodies were recovered, the other four are still in the wall. At the break-up of the Federation, Kariba remained in the joint possession of Zambia and Zimbabwe who still run the power station together.

and the achievement

The facts and figures are all on a gigantic scale. The dam wall is 126 metres high with a further 8 metres of foundations sunk into the bedrock. It is 24 metres wide at the base, and 12 metres wide and 633 metres long at the top. It contains 1,050,000 cubic metres of concrete and 11,000 tons of steel. There are six flood gates each 10 metres high, any one of which can raise the level of the river by 2.5 metres. To open even one means that advance warning must be given to those living downstream. They have all been opened together only twice—and once was at the project's opening. The lake is 290 km long and a maximum width of 32 km. Its maximum depth is 120 metres. All in all it is the fifth largest reservoir in the world. The top of the dam wall is a no man's land between Zimbabwe and Zambia; you are allowed on to have a look without going through border formalities.

Kariba Town

Kariba is billed as the Zimbabwean Riviera—a place of sun and sand where Zimbabweans go to play. They do, but as a visitor in search of the 'real' Africa be prepared to be disappointed. The town was built in the 1950s as a work camp to serve the people constructing the dam and running the power station. There isn't really a town as such, just a few small shops (one supermarket, one other shop, one chemist, one bank and a bunch of women selling crochet tablecloths) at Kariba Heights, up a very steep hill, and a line of hotels, the yacht club and marina strung out along the lakeshore. I spent two nights there on my last trip looking earnestly for the vibrant social life promised by the brochures. All I found was a drunken heap of white Zimbabweans surrounded by a mountain of empty beer cans.

Not exactly the centre of the universe

The Kariba Publicity Association can be contacted at PO Box 86, Kariba. Tel: 328.

Accommodation

All the **hotels** are on the water's edge and except for the Caribbea Bay there is little to choose between them.

Caribbea Bay: Built on Mediterranean resort lines, with a maze of white, rough-plastered 'casitas', lots of noise, lots of young people and plenty to do. Don't go near it if you're looking for peace and quiet. Entry to the complex is Z$2 a day if you're not staying there. PO Box 120, Kariba. Tel: 2453/4 Fax: 2765. Or book through the Zimbabwe Sun Central Reservations Office, Harare (see Appendix). dix).

*Cutty Sark****: Smallish, pleasant family hotel with all the amenities you would need and nice grounds. The day-trip boats leave from here. No beach. PO Box 80, Kariba. Tel: 2321. Telex: 41298 ZW. Or book through Goodwood's Central Reservations Office, PO Box 1490, Harare. Tel: 705081. Telex: 24164 ZW.

*Lake View Inn****: Most sedate of the hotels in town. Very quiet and peaceful with superb views out over the lake. Lovely gardens, but a very steep walk to the water's edge. PO Box 100, Kariba. Tel: 2411/2. Or book through the Zimbabwe Sun Central Reservations Office, Harare.

Kariba Breezes Hotel. part of the Kariba Breezes Marina complex. Pleasant, reasonably simple and reasonably cheap. PO Box 3, Kariba. Tel: 2433/4. Telex: 4826 ZW.

Camping.

Caribbea Bay: There is a camping and caravan site next to the resort with full facilities and access to the restaurants, entertainment, etc, within the main complex. There is a small shop near the hotel reception desk. PO Box 120, Kariba. Tel: 2454.

Mopani Bay Camping and Caravan Park: Space for 55 caravans and full facilities, 2.5 km east of Kariba town on the Makuti Road. PO Box 130, Kariba. Tel: 22313.

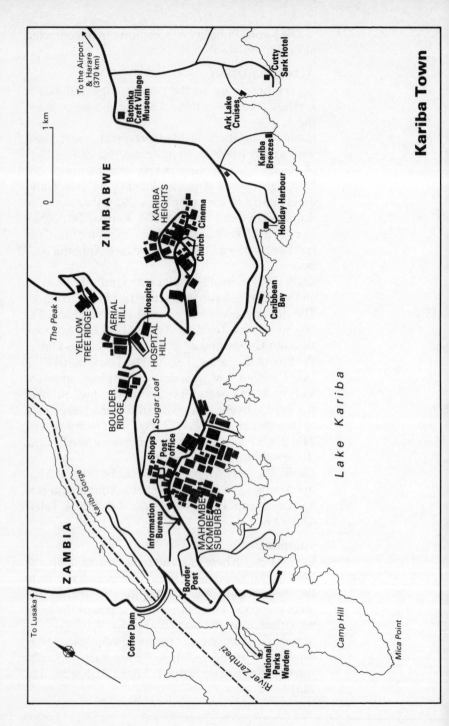

Kariba Town

MOTH Holiday Resort. Pleasant camping and chalets, situated near the Lake View Inn. Contact the Warden for bookings at PO Box 67, Kariba. Tel: 2809.

Things to See
Monument to Operation Noah.
As the lake flooded after the completion of the dam, thousands of animals were marooned on its many newly created islands. As the waters rose further, many of them were being drowned, too far now from the shore to hope to swim to safety. Rangers soon took to rescuing as many of the small animals as they could reach, ferrying them across to safety in their tiny boats. News of the animals' plight leaked out, the world's press took up the story, and public pressure forced the government to increase the size of the team from three to 57 rangers and trackers. They worked flat out, saving 4700 animals, large and small, in what became the largest and most famous animal rescue since the Ark. There is a monument to Operation Noah at Kariba Heights, giving details of the operation and those animals rescued.

Animals saved from drowning

St Barbara's Chapel.
Also at Kariba Heights is a small church built by the Italian construction workers in memory of 86 of their colleagues who died while building the dam wall. Its circular shape is that of a coffer dam, while the six surrounding pillars represent the six coffer dams built before the main wall. It is dedicated to St Barbara (the patron saint of engineers), St Joseph (the patron saint of carpenters) and Mary. There are also statues of St George of England (a copy of Donatello's masterpiece) and St Catherine of Italy to represent the involvement of Britain and Italy in the Kariba town and dam construction project. All the statues are made of Carrera marble. Pope Paul VI, formerly Archbishop of Milan, donated the tabernacle in 1964. A memorial stone lists the names of the dead.

Observation Point. This is the highest point in the area, with a magnificent view over town, lake and wall. There is a car park, tiny museum, gift shop and tea room. The man who runs it specialises in carving Tonga ceremonial sticks—beautiful, incredibly detailed poles, a bit larger than an ordinary walking stick— which tell the history of the Tonga people, local legends and even (his masterpiece) the entire history of Zimbabwe.

Things to Do
All activities centre on the lake, the closest thing Zimbabweans have to a sea.

Watersports. The Caribbea Bay Hotel (see above) is the centre of most activity in the area, with a swimming beach that they swear is kept clear of bilharzia. They also have kayaks, windsurfers, dinghies, paddleskis and waterskis for hire.

Cruises, charters and water safaris

Boats. There are day trips to Sanyati Gorge and Fothergill Island and afternoon and evening 'snooze cruises' along the lake shore, supposedly with the idea of seeing hippos. Don't count on it. Just lie back and enjoy the sun. Run by UTC from the Cutty Sark Hotel, Lake View Inn and Caribbean Bay. Motor cruisers and yachts are available for hire, as are facilities for mooring. Among the numerous charterers are:
Lake Safaris, PO Box 34, Kariba. Tel: 2474.
Kariba Yacht Safaris, 6 Fairfield Road, Hatfield, Harare. Tel: 50305.
Sea Quest, PO Box 36, Kariba. Tel: 2474.
Kariba Breezes Marina, PO Box 15, Kariba. Tel: 2475.
For lake safaris and fishing trips you can try the above and also the following:
Canoeing Safaris, PO Box 2625, Harare. Tel: 26513. Telex: 4187 ZW.
Cutty Sark Hotel (Safari Connection), PO Box 80, Kariba. Tel: 2321.

Fishing. There are 41 species of fish in the lake, of which only one, the karpenta, or fresh water sardine, has been introduced. The fishing is excellent, both from the shore for smaller species such as the delicious Kariba bream or from boats for larger game fish such as the fighting tiger fish. Other common species are vundu, chessa, nkupe, bottlenose, barbel and Hunyani salmon. Fishing along the entire length of the Zambezi is free and year-round. The Zimbabwe Tourist Board puts out an excellent pamphlet on fishing in the country, describing the main fish to be found and the best places to find them.

Excellent fishing, but don't get caught by a crocodile

Be on the lookout for crocodiles if fishing off the shore.

Other activities. The Kariba Crocodile Farm (PO Box 55, Kariba. Tel: 2338) is situated several miles east of Kariba Town, near the airport. For details about crocodile farming, see under Victoria Falls.

There is a casino every evening at Caribbea Bay.

The Charara Safari Area is a sort of mini game park. It is the only one easily accessible by road from the town, but it does not offer much.

WEST ALONG LAKE KARIBA

Many people don't bother to stay in Kariba town at all but head off to the many small camps or reserves scattered around this inland sea. Some are so isolated that they can only be reached by boat or plane. Others are accessible by road but usually only during the dry season and even then only in a four-wheel drive vehicle.

Close to paradise

This is truly the way to fall off the end of the world into something that comes very close to paradise. And you can be as sociable or anti-social as you like, either sitting sipping a drink in a luxury lodge as you watch the sunset or camping right out in the bush with nothing but the crickets to keep you company.

Matusadona National Park

The park occupies an area of 1407 sq km between the Umi and Sanyati Rivers on the south side of the lake.

Getting to Matusadona by road ...

It is extremely difficult to get to by road but can be reached from either Victoria Falls or Karoi, 87 km southeast of Kariba. Take the Harare-Lusaka road and turn left across the Urungwe Communal Land 8 km north of Karoi. 115 km later you'll cross the Sanyati River; follow the Binga road for 62 km more, then turn right to Tashinga, which is a further 82 km. This is the Park Headquarters. After leaving the Harare-Lusaka road you will be on gravel; the last stretch is extremely rough and not suitable for ordinary saloon cars—it can be totally impassable even with four-wheel drive during the rainy season. Only a third of the park is accessible, the remainder being very wild and rugged and having no roads.

or by air or water

Alternatively there is a small airstrip 800 metres long at Tashinga Camp, licensed to category II. Or you can easily reach Tashinga by boat, either from Bumi (14 km away) or Kariba (48 km).

NB: There is no fuel for sale within the park. The nearest is an intermittent supply at Bumi. The nearest garage which can do any repairs is at Kariba. Nor is there any help to carry equipment to the campsite if you arrive by air or boat.

National Park Accommodation
Camping. The main park campsite is at *Tashinga*, on the lake shore. It has full facilities including hot water and firewood. Camping equipment is available for hire on this site only.

There is also a camping ground for up to six tents at *Sanyati*, with hot and cold water and toilets.

Lodges. There are three permanent remote camps for exclusive hire. Each consists of two sleeping units with two rooms (sleeping up to six people in each) and bathroom, and a communal living area with kitchen, dining room, laundry and store room. A maximum of 12 people can use the camp at any one time. You must take in all food and drinking water. Cutlery, etc, for ten is provided.

Booking for all accommodation is through the National Parks Central Booking Office, Harare.

Private Accommodation near the Park
*Bumi Hills****: A private safari lodge and game park at the luxury end of the scale. Access is by small plane, the 'Orange Blossom' from Kariba Airport (it meets the Harare flight daily). The main Bumi Hills Lodge is a small, comfortable, laid-back hotel. The rooms are strung out along the hillside, each with a private balcony, to give the best possible view out over the lake and the flood plain beside it—one of the best game viewing spots in the reserve. There are day and night tours by open-topped Land Rover or boat or on foot, and several hides. For those who want to get further away, they run a camp called Water Wilderness—two houseboats on the Chura River with comfortable accommodation and well-stocked with food and drink. You will be accompanied by a ranger and

can spend the days walking. Run by Zimbabwe Sun. PO Box 41, Kariba. Tel: 2353. Or book through Central Reservations Office, Harare.

Fothergill Island: Named after Rupert Fothergill, the man behind Operation Noah, this island just off Matusadona National Park still has a large game population of its own. It has been developed as an upmarket safari camp using open grass huts as sleeping accommodation and with guided tours in open Land Rovers, boats and on foot. Access is by air, and the small plane is available at other times for private charter. They also have a houseboat just off the Matusadona coast and run walking safaris in the game park. Run by Kazangula Safaris, Post Bag 2081, Kariba. Tel: 2253. Telex: 4008 ZW.

Tiger Bay: Another relaxed but very comfortable safari resort on the Ume River with 12 thatched chalets with en suite bathrooms. Access is by air. The accent is on fishing, with boats and tackle for hire. Enquiries to Zambezi River Safaris, PO Box 102, Kariba. Tel: 2569.

Spurwing Island: Another private, luxury island complex, this time under canvas. Informal, friendly and reasonably priced, with knowledgeable staff and good game viewing. Enquiries to P.Bag 101, Kariba. Tel: 2466.

VICTORIA FALLS

Geology

A volanic past

One hundred and fifty million years ago the whole of southern Africa was wracked by intense volcanic activity, and a 300-metre thick lava field spread over the land, hardening to form a dense basalt. As it cooled and solidified, the rock shrank and cracked, forming fissures running both north-south and east-west that were later eroded by the weather into wide crevasses. Millions of years later the area along this stretch became a lake, and softer deposits of clay and lime were laid on top of the basalt. The lake dried and the surface layer eroded away, leaving only the fissures filled with the softer material which eventually compacted to form limestone.

Still later, the Zambezi carved its course through the soft limestone but could not so easily erode the basalt on either side of the fissures. At its confluence with the Matetsi, the Zambezi fell 250 metres into the deep Matetsi Valley, forming a waterfall 100 km downstream from the present falls. The constant rush of water eroded this first falls, creating along its course (which was the bed of an ancient east-west fissure) a series of retreating rapids and falls that ran from 2.5 km above the present falls to 8 km below them. This is the strip now called the Batoka Gorge, some of the most dangerous white water in the world. The line can be seen clearly from any high vantage point or from the air.

Creation of the
Batoka Gorge

As the line of the falls retreated, it came alongside a north-south fissure and eroded the limestone from this before retreating along the east-west fissure once again. This north-south crevasse created a broad fall similar to the present Victoria Falls, although several kilometres downstream. In the course of time there have been eight of these falls, the biggest waterfalls in the world, each linked by the narrower east-west course of the river. The

Victoria Falls from a light aircraft

The heart of the flow Devil's Cataract (the first of the falls reached from the main path) is far deeper and more intense than the rest of the flow, and it is thought that this is the start of the river's retreat towards the next north-south fissure. On the route of that new retreat there will be a narrow if intensely powerful flow before the river finds the next north-south fissure and creates a new broad fall.

Victoria Falls is between 61 and 105 metres high and 1688 metres wide. About 545 million litres of water pours over it every minute in flood season, sending spray some 500 metres into the air.

History

Livingstone is credited as being the first white man to see the falls, although there are several Afrikaans families who claim that their ancestors hunted regularly in the area and knew about them long before Livingstone's arrival in November 1855. Having failed for the second time to establish a mission at Chobe, Livingstone started along the river, looking for a route through to the east coast. He had already heard of the falls by their local name Mosi Oa Tunya or 'The Smoke That Thunders' and had left the river to travel along the north bank and so avoid the rapids which led to the main fall. but his curiosity got the better of him, and on 16 November he was taken by canoe to the northern end of an island on the lip of the falls, now known as Livingstone Island. The spectacle before him moved him to a rare flight of fancy; the entry in his diary, 'On sights as beautiful as this Angels in their flight must have gazed', has become one of travel's most often used quotations. When he recovered himself, he claimed the falls for the crown and named them after his Queen.

Livingstone's flight of fancy

A bronze memorial statue to Livingstone now stands in a clearing beside Devil's Cataract, facing Livingstone Island.

Viewing the Falls

Roar and spray

From the moment you come within a few kilometres of the falls the air is filled by a dull roar and a cloud of spray reaches up hundreds of metres like a beacon. But at ground level you get no further warning until you are almost on the brink of the gorge, as a thin band of rainforest fed by the spray hides the river behind a dense green curtain.

There is a car park with ample space, a map board and an information centre a couple of hundred metres from the falls. A pleasanter approach however is down a small path, about a kilometre long, that leads through the bush from the Victoria Falls and Mkasa Sun hotels. As you cover the last few yards you will begin to feel the effects of the spray, a constant shower of rain that will have you wringing litres of water from your clothes within minutes. If you mind getting wet (it is impossible to remain completely dry, no matter what you wear), there are plastic raincoats for hire at Z$1 a time from the hut by the car park. Do make sure that camera equipment is well

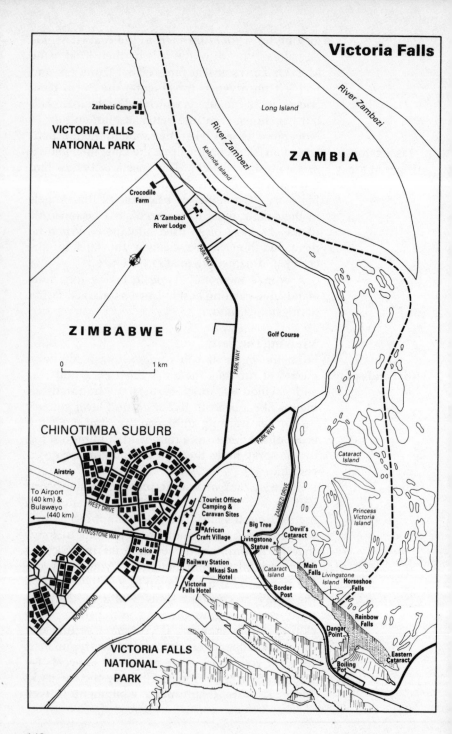

Victoria Falls

Zambezi Camp

VICTORIA FALLS
NATIONAL PARK

River Zambezi

Long Island

River Zambezi

Kalunda Island

ZAMBIA

Crocodile Farm

A 'Zambezi River Lodge

PARK WAY

ZIMBABWE

Golf Course

PARK WAY

0   1 km

CHINOTIMBA SUBURB

Airstrip

To Airport
(40 km) &
Bulawayo
(440 km)

WEST DRIVE

LIVINGSTONE WAY

Police

PARK WAY

ZAMBEZI DRIVE

Cataract Island

Tourist Office/
Camping &
Caravan Sites

African Craft Village

Big Tree

Devil's
Cataract

Princess
Victoria
Island

Livingstone
Statue

Railway Station

Mkasi Sun
Hotel

Cataract Island

Main
Falls

Livingstone
Island

Horseshoe
Falls

PIONEER ROAD

Victoria
Falls Hotel

Border
Post

Rainbow
Falls

Danger
Point

VICTORIA FALLS
NATIONAL
PARK

Eastern
Cataract

Boiling
Pot

housed in waterproof plastic before you venture near.

There are five falls altogether. **Devil's Cataract** is the nearest to the car park, a narrow section, but with the deepest and most powerful flow. There are two main viewing points here. **Chain Walk** is down a steep stairway in the side of the gorge. From here you can get the most incredible sense of the force of the water, which is so close you can almost reach out and touch it. Don't wear slippery shoes as the steps are stone and permanently wet and there would be no chance of surviving if you fell over the edge. The **Livingstone Memorial Statue** is situated in a clearing beside the head of the Devil's Cataract. You can see little of the main falls from here, but it is the only point at which you can get a clear view unimpeded by the spray, and from a relatively dry standpoint. It is also the best place for photographing the sunrise. I recommend getting up early enough to do the trek while it is still dark (a flashlight is essential). The spray turns blood red in the pre-dawn light, and is a sight to stop you breathing. Then slowly, slowly it fades to a delicate shell-pink which stains the whole, steaming river, before the sun appears on the opposite bank adding orange and gold. I also went down here in the full moon, jumping at every pair of eyes I saw in the flashlight beam (large numbers of spring hares, two bushbuck and a baboon), but only next morning seeing the large pugmarks (leopard) that had crossed my footprints on the dirt track. It was a sight well worth the near heart attack, but don't go on your own.

Cataract Island, which is criss-crossed by a number of small rivulets, separates Devil's Cataract from the **Main Falls**, the first of the wide sheets of water that make up the largest and most famous portion of the falls. To see these, backtrack along the path and turn in the opposite direction to Livingstone, along a path that leads through the rainforest. There is no uninterrupted view of the falls

The falls by dawn and moonlight

A walk along the line of falls

as you walk, but there are a number of short paths leading to viewing points along the rim. **Livingstone Island** separates Main Falls from **Horseshoe Falls** (so called because of the deep curve in the cliff), **Rainbow Falls**, and the **Eastern Cataract** (the farthest of the five).

Along this stretch the spray is at its densest. When the river is at its height you will see very little but a solid wall of white with an occasional tantalising break as the breeze picks up. It is very dramatic, but the best time to visit is actually during September and October, at the end of the dry season, when the river and therefore the spray is at its lowest ebb. Then you will have an almost unimpeded view, both of the falls and of the numerous rainbows which are almost always present.

At the far end of the south rim is a lookout point over the Eastern Cataract, a falls that can almost dry up in winter. This is **Danger Point**. Here you have finally left the rainforest behind you and can stand basking in sunlight with a view both of the falls on one side and the river gorge and bridge on the other. A short walk further takes you to the final viewing point near the bridge, from where you can look down into the aptly named **Boiling Pot**, a whirling cauldron where all the water that has been hurled over the falls is channelled, protesting, into the narrow gorge.

Rhodes' bridge   It was Rhodes who declared that a **bridge**, part of his beloved Cape to Cairo railway, should be built across this second gorge so that passengers could feel the spray and see the falls in all their glory as they crossed. This was done, though he died before the railway reached this far. The railway reached the falls in 1904 and on 1 April 1905 the final middle section of the bridge was slotted into place. It is both a road and rail link and holds both Zimbabwean and Zambian border posts. There is another path that leads back to the car park from here, behind the rainforest, in the dry. It is also a very pretty route, and there are usually plenty of small animals such as monkeys, buck and birds to see.

The Flight of Angels

Appreciating the full scope of the falls

This short flight over the Falls is an essential—not cheap but well worth saving for. The plane is a six-seater Piper Aztec, its only drawback being that it flies too high (about 3000 metres) and too fast to allow you to open the windows. Operated by United Air Charters, the flight departs from an old airstrip 6 km from the Falls Village. The flight-path makes a beeline for the falls and spends most of the time circling to provide the best view for photographers. And the view is wonderful—you are high enough to see over the spray and take in the entire massive width of Victoria Falls.

United Air Charters also runs a 30-minute Spray-view Safari in the early morning and late afternoon, taking in some game viewing, and the Zambezi Sky Safari which lasts 75 minutes. There is a courtesy bus to the airstrip, and flights will depart at any time as long as there are at least four passengers. Booking through UTC. Advance booking is essential.

The Town

Although the pioneer column into Zambia came past this area and even camped near the falls for a while, there was no permanent settlement until the railway—and the tourists—arrived in 1905. The village, which now has a population of about 8000, is almost wholly a tourist-based creation, with several souvenir shops as well as food shops, bank, post office, etc.

The Victoria Falls Publicity Association runs a tourist office on Parkway, in the centre of the village. PO Box 97, Victoria Falls. Tel: 4202.
UTC have a central office in the Zimbank Building, Livingstone Way (Tel: 4267/8), as well as desks in the main hotels. *Safari Secretarial Services*, based at the Sprayview Hotel (Tel: 4344) act as booking agents for game-viewing trips on horseback, run by

Zambezi Horse Trials, while *Safari Office Services* on Parkway (Tel: 471/2/3) act for a couple of small companies offering escorted game-viewing trips on foot.

Things to See Apart from Victoria Falls

The upside down tree

The Big Tree. Local legend has it that the baobab tree somehow offended the gods, who in their fury uprooted it and struck it back in the ground upside down. And indeed its spindly branches, bare for most of the year, do look more like roots. It is a deciduous tree with a swollen, spongy, water-storing trunk and smooth grey bark. Large white flowers blossom in October and November, followed by large woody fruit with a velvety olive green skin. Cracked open, the creamy pulp, from which cream of tartar is derived, is good to eat, and the young leaves can be eaten as vegetables and the seeds roasted. The bark is sometimes used for rope, nets and clothing. The baobab is common in low rainfall areas at low altitude.

This particular Big Tree, on the road leading round to the Falls Car Park, is the grand-daddy of them all, about 20 metres around the trunk and 25 metres high. Even by the turn of the century it was large enough to be a useful landmark and was the campsite of the early pioneers, later becoming the traditional meeting place for anyone in the area. Fenced off now and protected as a tourist sight, it is still growing.

Traditional dwellings

African Craft Village. This open air museum of local culture is right in the centre of the village. There is a modest entry fee which includes a guidebook. Inside the grass fence are a series of traditional huts from each of the main tribal groups in the country—all original dwellings that have been moved to the site and authentically furnished. Amongst them are a Venda chief's hut, highly decorated and with separate areas for the kitchen, bathroom and guard posts; a bushman shelter; and a Nyanga funerary hut. They are all well labelled, but there are also guided tours at regular intervals through the day. If you want to check on your own well being, there are two witch doctors on site ready to read your fortune.

Crocodile Farm. Situated opposite the A'Zambezi River Lodge about 4 km from the village centre, Spencer's Creek is one of the largest of several crocodile farms in the country and probably the best laid out from the tourist's point of view. Each year the farm is licenced to collect 2500 eggs, as crocodiles will rarely breed in captivity. In return, five percent are restored to the wild once they are about a metre long (three to four years old). Eggs and baby crocs are extremely vulnerable to predators (including older crocodiles) so this means that about double the number are being returned to the wild as would have survived naturally. You are shown crocodiles at all stages of development from several centimetres long (which you may be allowed to hold) to Big Daddy—at over five metres one of the largest crocodiles in captivity.

Raising baby crocodiles

There are also all sorts of amazing facts—such as when a crocodile whips its head round to attack it moves at up to 250 kph, or that, more comfortingly, crocodiles only need to eat once every two months and can survive for up to 17 months without food. They only need to breath every couple of minutes and can live for up to 100 years.

Snake Park. The Zambezi Taxidermy and Snake Park is right in the centre of the village. Turn left by the Post Office onto Adam Stander Drive and it's the last building on the left. There is a wide variety of snakes, including some of the country's most dangerous, which you can see being 'milked' of their poison at various times through the day. And as the name suggests, you will also see a lot of dead animals and can be shown over the workshop to see how taxidermy is done. Tel: 4236.

Game Park. The whole area from the edge of the airport to the river is national park, but around the edge of the settlement there is also a game park. It is very small and, if you have already been to any of the others such as Mana Pools or Hwange, rather disappointing.

The **Sundowner or 'Booze Cruise'** normally leaves between 4.30 and 5.30 from a mooring beside the A'Zambezi River Lodge upstream from the rapids, shifting its timing with the season to catch the sunset. It earned its nickname years ago when the price of the ticket included as much booze as you could swallow—and most white Rhodesians took the opportunity to get totally blitzed. No more; now you have to pay for your drinks. The boat has an **Evening** enclosed lower deck, but everyone makes for the **drinks for** top deck where tables are laid out and waiters serve **passengers...** the drinks. The boat chugs slowly upstream to Kandahar Island, past scenery that looks like a Tarzan film set—tangled jungles of monkey ropes and the straight silhouettes of ivory palms—getting there just in time for the scarlet and gold sunset, a superlative display of natural pyrotechnics. And then, as the sun finally disappears, you turn slowly **and animals** and drift back downstream, scouring the banks for the local wildlife coming down for an evening drink. There are also morning and afternoon departures if you can't get onto the evening one. Book ahead, through UTC.

Evening Entertainment
The **African Spectacular** is held in a grass enclosure in the grounds of the Victoria Falls Hotel each evening at 7pm. As the sun disappears, the mournful howl of a kudu horn bugle splits the air, gradually joined by the hollow, complicated rhythms of the drums. You walk through a craft shop cluttered with strange masks and carvings, smelling of wood and straw, into the arena where a couple of traditional mud huts and a huge fire face the seating. By the fire are seated the Makishi drummers, their bare chests glistening with reflected flame. The women cluster behind them to form the

Masked dancers

chorus, not allowed by tradition to dance themselves. The Makishi dancers traditionally mask themselves from head to toe in skin-tight, brightly coloured stripes and huge wooden face masks, so they are unrecognisable even to their families. The dances act out family quarrels, the behaviour of animals, hunting expeditions and ancestor worship, the mood switching from uproarious laughter to almost religious awe.

The Shangaan, who share the programme, are a warrior people and their dances are those of ritual— a boy's circumcision ceremony, victory celebrations and dances designed to terrify the enemy before a battle. They dress in goat skin loin cloths, with bands of fleece around their calves and arms, stamping and yelling until the dust swirls around them and the ground shakes. The programme is simple, lasting about an hour, with plenty of humour and explanations at each stage of the meaning behind the dance to come. It is a purely commercial show, but great fun and well worth the entry fee.

Most people gravitate towards the Mkasa Sun Hotel later in the evening, as this is the home of the **Victoria Falls Casino**—almost as large a draw to the area, especially amongst Zimbabweans, as the falls themselves. It is not particularly smart, lounge suit rather than dinner jacket, and fairly casual, designed for a pleasant evening's entertainment rather than for hooking as much money as possible from hardened gamblers. Most people will be able to afford the stakes and need not feel foolish if they are playing low.

Getting Around

The **airport** is about 40 km away from the falls, on the far side of the Game Park, but Air Zimbabwe run a bus that meets all flights.

Car hire is available, but book from Harare before arriving as the fleet is small and it is virtually impossible to get one without endless delays and expensive telexes back to Harare.

149

Once in the village you can get around fairly easily on **foot**, or by using the **courtesy transport** laid on by the hotels, or by taking a **UTC tour**. These take in such 'musts' as the 'Booze Cruise' and the Flight of Angels. The garage on the corner as you turn off towards the Victoria Falls and Mkasa Sun hotels hires out **bicycles**. There is a 5-km path along the banks of the river, which is a very pleasant cycle ride with beautiful scenery and the possibility of seeing all sorts of wildlife. Another easy cycle ride is to cross into Zambia for the day.

Easy bicycling

Accommodation

Hotels. All the hotels in the area are very comfortable, but none of them are cheap, starting at about Z$80 a night for bed and breakfast, single. If you're on a tight budget you will have to go self-catering.

Victoria Falls Hotel****: The oldest of the hotels in the town, this started as a simple building of wood and corrugated iron in 1904. Now an imposing classical building, it is one of the best hotels in southern Africa, with a superb view over the falls and the bridge. PO Box 10, Victoria Falls. Tel: 4203. Or book through the Zimbabwe Sun Hotels Central Reservation Office. Tel: Harare 736644.

Makasa Sun Hotel****: Much newer, but also very good quality, and home to the Victoria Falls Casino. PO Box 90, Victoria Falls. Tel: 4275. Or book through the Zimbabwe Sun Hotel Central Reservations Office, Harare (see above).

A' Zambezi River Lodge***: A sprawling, thatched and very attractive complex about 4 km upstream from the falls, right on the river bank. Run by Zimbabwe Tourist Development Corporation, PO Box 130, Victoria Falls. Tel: 4561. Telex: 51657 ZW. Or book through ZTDC Central Reservations in Harare. Tel: 793666.

Rainbow Hotel***: A recently refurbished hotel in the centre of the village with Moorish architecture. Also run by the ZTDC (see above). PO Box 150, Victoria Falls. Tel: 4585. Fax: 4653. Or book through ZTDC in Harare.

Sprayview Motel**: The smallest of the hotels in the area, this is also the cheapest and furthest from the falls, out near the old aerodrome. Tel: 4344.

Self-catering and camping. There is a Rest Camp in the centre of the village with a selection of dormitory accommodation, one and two-bedroomed chalets and a camping site. It is run by the Town Council which also provides a 60-space **caravan site** on the riverbank, 3 km from the village. Both are kept in excellent condition with full facilities. Write to the Secretary, Victoria Falls Town Council, PO Box 41, Victoria Falls, for details or to book.

The National Parks Authority has some **self-catering lodges** sleeping up to six people at Zambezi Camp, 6 km upstream from the falls. These are within the game reserve so transport is essential. It also has three remote and very simple fishing camps, at Kandahar, which is open all year, at Sansima and at Mpala Jena (open from May to October). As for all other National Parks properties, obtain details from and make bookings through their Central Booking Office, Harare.

Eating
If you want to eat out you will have to eat at the hotels or, if your budget won't stretch, at the Wimpey! In high season the Victoria Falls Hotel does an excellent braai every evening very cheaply and a buffet lunch, which is more expensive, but you can eat as much as you want. Otherwise you will have to cook your own. The general shops are in the centre of the village near the information office.

HWANGE NATIONAL PARK

One of Africa's great game reserves

Hwange is the biggest of Zimbabwe's game reserves and one of the last great wildlife reserves of Africa. It covers an area of 14,650 sq km in the northwest corner of the country and contains 107 species of animals and 410 species of birds. The best time of year for game spotting is between May and December when the vegetation isn't so lush and water is scarcer, bringing the animals into greater concentrations.

Getting to the Park

By car. Access to the park is from the main Bulawayo-Victoria Falls Road. Specific details on getting to each camp are given in the accommodation section.

By rail. The nearest station is Dete, 24 km from Main Camp. UTC provides transport to the park, but this must be arranged in advance as the train arrives at 1am.

By air. There is a scheduled service to Hwange National Park Aerodrome from where UTC can provide transport. There is a small unlicenced airstrip at Main Camp. You must get permission to land in advance from the Provincial Warden. Tel: Dete 222.

Getting Around within the Park

Once in the park you must have your own car or take guided tours. Hitchhiking is forbidden within the park boundaries.

By car. There are 482 km of road within the park, though only one short stretch is tarred and some of the roads are impassable during the rainy season. Ask at the camps for advice on which are the best routes to take, where you are most likely to see game and how long your journey will take. There is a speed limit of 40 kph. As you have either to leave the park or report into a camp before 6pm each evening, you must leave by 12 noon if travelling between Main and Robins Camps, by 2pm between Main Camp and Sinamatella and by 3pm between Sinamatella and Robins. You are also **Keeping in** asked to keep the park authorities informed as to **touch** where you are going so they can sent out search parties should you go missing. More detailed maps of the area around each camp are available from the warden's office. Petrol and diesel are available at Robins and Main Camps, but there are no maintenance facilities closer than Hwange town. No vehicles weighing more than 3 tonnes, caravans and trailers with space for over 20 people, open vehicles or motorbikes are allowed into the park.

Tours. UTC has an office at the Hwange Safari Lodge and runs regular game viewing tours that will also pick up passengers at Main Camp. The hotel also runs its own tours, including night tours in areas just outside the park boundaries.

Accommodation
Within the park.
Main Camp: The main turn-off is by the 264.5 km peg on the Bulawayo-Victoria Falls Road. A tarred road about 15 km long leads to the park boundary, not far from the camp. This is the largest of the camps and there is a variety of accommodation here, including some one- and two-bedroomed cottages with their own bathrooms, though cooking and dining are communal; some larger lodges with full cooking facilities; and chalets with braai areas only. There is also a small camping and caravan site, a restaurant that serves take-away snacks, a bar and a store that is open from 7.45 to 10am, 12 to 2pm and 3 to 7pm. The camp is open all year. Post bag DT 5776, Dete. Tel: 371.
Sinamatella: The turn-off from the Bulawayo-Victoria Falls Road is just south of Hwange town. The camp is about 45 km further on, along a gravel road, via the Mbala lodge in the Deka Safari Area. It is

Elephants and antelopes in Hwange National Park

situated on a high plateau that gives excellent views of the surrounding area. Sinamatella has one- and two-bedroomed cottages, lodges and chalets, a camp site and a small store. The camp is open all year. Post Bag WK 5941, Hwange. Tel: Hwange 44522.

Bumbusi and Lukosi Camps: Both are 'exclusive', meaning your party will be the only one there. Both are in the Sinimatella area and will house up to 12 people. They are fully equipped, but you will have to take in all your own supplies. Four-wheel drive is recommended for Bumbusi in the rainy season.

Robins Camp and Nantwich Lodges: Access is via a gravel road turn-off from the main Bulawayo-Victoria Falls Road 48 km south of Victoria Falls. It is about 70 km from the turning to the camp. The Nantwich Lodges are 11 km from Robins Camp along a gravel road. Robins Camp is closed from 1 November to 30 April; you should check on the condition of the road before setting off at other times. The Nantwich Lodges are normally open all year. Robins Camp has only basic chalets with communal facilities. It is lit only between dusk and 10pm. Post Bag WK 5936, Hwange. Tel: Hwange 70220.

Deka Exclusive Camp: 25 km west of Robins Camp, Deka is fully serviced and equipped for up to 12 people. The access road is only available for four-wheel-drive.

Further details are available and bookings for any of the camps can be made through the National Parks Central Reservations Office, Harare (see Appendix).

Outside the park.

Hwange Safari Lodge***: This only has three stars but in my opinion is worthy of more. Run by Zimbabwe Sun on the boundary of the National Park along the road to Main Camp, the lodge has an extensive game reserve of its own, offering some good viewing without leaving the grounds. There is also a Bush Camp with grass huts and tree houses for evenings around the bonfire or under the stars, with some night drives thrown in. Food and atmosphere are designed for those who look for a little 'colonial' luxury in their safaris. PO Box DT 5792, Dete. Tel: Dete 331/2. Telex: ZW 51602. Or book through Zimbabwe Sun Central Booking Office, Harare (see Appendix).

Gwaai River Hotel*: A simpler but still pleasant hotel 32 km from the park, just off the main Victoria Falls-Bulawayo Road near the Gwaai River Bridge. PO Box 9, Gwaai. Tel: Dete 3400.

Sikumi Tree Lodge: A camp with accommodation in 12 large thatched tree houses plus a few chalets at ground level. They will meet the Harare plane and offer game-viewing trips in vehicles or on foot. Post Bag 5779, Dete. Tel: 2105. Telex: 51604 ZW.

SECTION 4: MATABELELAND AND THE SOUTH

Bulawayo and Environs

Khami Ruins

Matobo National Park

Masvingo and Environs

Kyle Dam and Lake

Great Zimbabwe

Gonarezhou National Park

BULAWAYO AND ENVIRONS

Getting There

By air. There are regular flights to Bulawayo from Harare via Gweru, and from Victoria Falls and Johannesburg. The airport is 22 km from town along the Queens Road, but Air Zimbabwe operates a regular bus service to the City terminal, Treger House, Jason Moyo St, between 11th and 12th Avenues. PO Box 1000. Tel: 72051.

By rail. There are rail links with Botswana and South Africa, and with Victoria Falls and Harare, all with regular services. The station is at the junction of 14th Avenue and Lobengula Street. Tel: 72311.

By road. Good tarred **roads** lead to Bulawayo from all other major centres in Zimbabwe as well as from the Botswana border at Plumtree and the South African border at Beit Bridge. Travelling lonely roads in this area is not recommended after dusk as there is still some trouble in the area. You will probably meet police roadblocks.

There are regular **coach services** to Bulawayo from Johannesburg, Harare, Victoria Falls and Masvingo. The coach terminals are at the City Car Park, Leopold Takawira Ave; Bulawayo Sun Hotel, Josiah Tongogawa Street and Tenth Avenue; and Zimbabwe Omnibus Company, Lobengula Street and Sixth Avenue. Contact the Bulawayo Publicity Association for times and prices.

Getting Around

Taxis. There are several taxi ranks within the city. Tel: 60666, 61933, 72454, 60154 or 60704.

Car hire. There are several car hire firms within the city. See the Appendix.

Local buses. The terminal for the northern, eastern and southern suburbs is at the City Hall, Eighth Avenue, between Fife St and Robert Mugabe Way. Tel: 67172. Timetables are available from the terminal. The terminal for the western suburbs is on the corner of Lobengula Street and Sixth Avenue. There are frequent services, but don't expect smart, comfortable transport.

History of Bulawayo

Bulawayo is one of the oldest and historically most important of Zimbabwe's towns. There has been settlement in the area for thousands of years, but it gained new prominence in 1868 when Lobengula inherited the Matabele throne from his father and moved his capital to the site of the present-day city. John Moffat, who was already running a mission at Inyati, was allowed to open another in Bulawayo in 1870 though he continued to have little success in making converts to Christianity. A Jesuit mission, now ruined, was established in 1879; its first convert was an Ndebele leper. A few other whites, traders and hunters, built houses in the area during Lobengula's reign.

Matabele capital

The royal kraal was situated just outside the present city centre, and it was here in 1888 that Alan Rudd's negotiations with the king led to the colonisation of the country.

For three years after the colonisation of Mashonaland an uneasy truce existed between the Matabele and the white settlers, but in June 1893 the situation flared into war. While Lobengula sent his armies to the Mashonaland border, a second white army, coming up from Bechuanaland, destroyed the royal kraal and forced the king to flee. Bulawayo became the Matabele headquarters of the British South Africa Company and for a while seemed set to take over from Salisbury as capital. The settlers ran into severe trouble in late 1896 when the warlike Ndebele rose again, and were in danger of starvation under siege conditions until Rhodes intervened to negotiate a peace settlement.

The Town

War between whites and Matabele

Today the town has a population of nearly 600,000, most of whom live in the 'high density' suburbs, leaving the centre as a small, peaceful country town with wide, tree-lined streets, low white buildings and a relaxed pace. The climate is much drier here than in Harare, as the town is on the edge of the Kalahari sands, but Bulawayo is an oasis of irrigation with lush parks and brightly coloured gardens. It is the only town in Zimbabwe of any size, other than Harare with which there has always been intense rivalry. Bulawayo remains the capital of Matabeleland.

The office of the Bulawayo Publicity Association is in the City Hall, on Fife Street, between Leopold Takawira Avenue and Eighth Avenue. PO Box 861, Bulawayo. Tel: 60867.

Things to See in Bulawayo

Centenary Park and Central Park. These are adjacent to each other and cover a total of 45 hectares

Shady retreat

between Samuel Parirenyatwa Street and Park Road. It is a wonderfully luxuriant, cool, green and shady area. The theatre, museum and camping site are all within Centenary Park as well as an aviary, small game enclosure, miniature railway, swimming pool and children's playground.

In Central Park, on the corner of Leopold Takawira Avenue, is Zimbabwe's largest ornamental fountain, Anniversary Fountain, erected in 1968 to commemmorate the city's 75th aniversary. It changes colour at night.

City Hall and Art Gallery. The City Hall is the centre of town and is surrounded by a flower and craft market and a bus terminal. As well as the Publicity Association offices, it houses the Bulawayo section of the National Archives, and in the foyer of the Council Chamber on the first floor are a collection of civic plate, Bulawayo's coat of arms and the Civic Honours Book. In the grounds is the Pioneer Well, the settlement's only water supply dur-

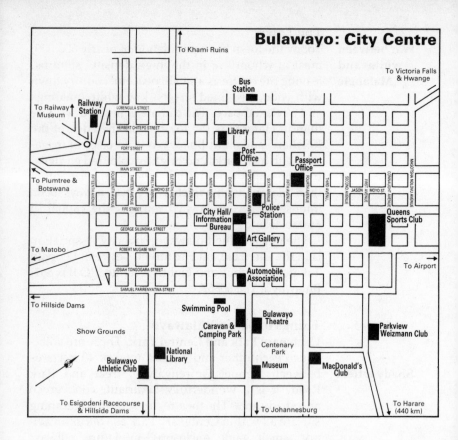

Bulawayo: City Centre

ing the Matabele Uprisings. Later filled in, it was rediscovered and reopened in 1951. The small art gallery is open daily from 10am to 5pm except on Mondays and Saturday afternoons. It is in the square formed by Leopold Takawira Avenue, Fife St and Robert Mugabe Way and Eighth Ave.

The best museum in the country

Natural History Museum. Founded in 1901 as the National Museum, this is by far the best museum in the country, worth an extended visit. It moved into its present building in Centenary Park in 1964. The mammal collection alone includes 75,000 specimens and is the largest in southern Africa and the eighth largest in the world, outside Canada and the USA. There are also major collections of birds, reptiles, fish and insects, galleries devoted to archaeology and anthropology, and a beautifully displayed geological section that includes a mock-up of a gold mine. Next to the museum is an open-air display of old mining equipment and memorabilia. The museum is also responsible for the care of all Zimbabwe's National Monuments. Arrangements can be made for visiting researchers to use the collections not on public display. Open daily from 9am to 5pm except Good Friday and Christmas Day. It is on the corner of Park Road and Leopold Takawira Avenue. PO Box 240, Bulawayo. Tel: 60045.

Railways Museum. The first train to reach Rhodesia arrived in Bulawayo on 19 October 1897. The town became the headquarters of the national railways as well as the chief junction and marshalling yard. The Railways Museum, near the station in the suburb of Raylton, has a selection of old steam locomotives, a refurbished 1904 passenger carriage, some old railway buildings and a variety of other relics of early railway days, and gives a detailed history of the railway in Zimbabwe. It is open from Tuesday to Friday from 9.30am to noon and 2 to 4pm; and on Sundays from 2 to 5pm. It is at the corner of Prospect Avenue and First Street, Raylton.

Old railway days

Mzilikaze Art and Crafts Centre. The idea for the centre began with some pottery classes in 1958; in 1963 the first part of the centre was opened. It now operates as a non-profit making but self-supporting welfare project with a commercial pottery employing 70 people producing high quality earthen and stoneware. It supports a free art school with 130 full-time students as well as adult evening classes and classes for up to 450 schoolchildren each week. Mzilikazi pottery is distinctive and pleasing. Visitors are welcome to tour the pottery, school, art gallery and seconds shop Monday to Friday from 10am to 12.30pm and 2 to 5pm. It is 4 km from the centre of town off the Old Falls Road near Mpilo Hospital,

Western Suburbs. PO Box 2034, Bulawayo. Tel: 67245.

Accommodation
There are no really upmarket hotels in Bulawayo.

Mid-range hotels.
Bulawayo Sun***: Corner of Tenth Avenue and Josiah Tongogara Street. Largest of the local hotels and very central, it is the most commonly used business hotel in the area. A little bit threadbare in places, but it has all that is needed, including secretarial facilities. Run by Zimbabwe Sun. PO Box 654, Bulawayo. Tel: 60101. Telex: ZW 33242. Fax: 61739. Or book through Zimbabwe Sun Central Reservations Office, Harare (see Appendix).

The Churchill Arms***: About 6 km from the centre of town on the corner of Matopos Road and Moffat Avenue. Mock-Tudor building, going for a cosy 'Olde Englishe' atmosphere. Run by Cresta Hotels. PO Box 9140, Hillside, Bulawayo. Tel: 41016. Or book via the Jameson Hotel, Harare.

Bulawayo Inn***: Away from the centre of town near the racetrack. Run by Zimbabwe Sun. Ascot Centre, PO Box AC88, Bulawayo. Tel: 72464. Telex: ZW33341. Fax: 76227.

Budget hotels.
Selborne**: Right in the heart of town on Leopold Takawira Avenue opposite the City Hall, this is the oldest of Bulawayo's hotels. The building is typically colonial. PO Box 219, Bulawayo. Tel: 65741.

New Royal**: Corner of Sixth Avenue and George Silundika Street. PO Box 1199, Bulawayo. Tel: 65764/5.

Grey's Inn**, 73 Robert Mugabe Way. PO Box 527, Bulawayo. Tel: 60121/2.

Plaza*, corner of 14th Avenue and Jason Moyo Street. PO Box 1521. Tel: 64280/1.

Cecil*, corner of Fife Street and Third Avenue. PO Box 274, Bulawayo. Tel: 60295.

Hostels.
Youth Hostel, corner of Townsend Road and Third Street. Tel: 76488.
YWCA, corner of Ninth Avenue and Lobengula Street. Tel: 60185. Accepts men and women.

Camping.
Municipal Caravan Park, in Centenary Park. Run by the City Council who pride themselves on the best campsite in Zimbabwe. Well laid out, plenty of shade and excellent facilities. Space for caravans and tents. PO Box 1641, Bulawayo. Tel: 75011.

What to See in the Surrounding Area

Chipingali Wildlife Orphanage is 23 km from Bulawayo along the Gwanda Road. This is a privately run trust set up to care for orphaned, sick or abandoned wildlife with the idea of returning them to the wild. A wide variety of animals including the big cats. Definitely worth visiting. Open every day except Mondays and Christmas Day. PO Box 1057, Bulawayo. Tel: 70764.

Cyrene Mission, 32 km from Bulawayo along the Plumtree Road. An Anglican mission whose church has been richly decorated with murals and carvings done by pupils. Ask the Publicity Bureau to arrange for you to visit.

Ancient ruins

Dhlo Dhlo. These small ruins are about 100 km from Bulawayo. To reach them take the main Harare Road. 50 km later a signed gravel road branches off and 32 km after that you will cross a concrete drift over a small river to reach a fork in the road. Take the left branch and you will reach the ruins 12 km later.

The ruins are small but sophisticated, the dry stone walling using herring bone and chevron designs as well as stones of differing colours in the patterning. It is thought that they are of a similar age to the main period at Great Zimbabwe—15th and 16th C AD—and a number of Portuguese artifacts found here show that it was in early contact with Europeans. Much of the site was damaged by treasure seekers at the end of the last century.

163

Gulubahwe Caves, 19 km beyond the Matopos Mission on the Gwanda Road. There are a number of cave paintings here, the most important of which is a multi-coloured snake, about 4.5 metres long with a number of humans and animals riding on its back. The snake is a sacred symbol to the local Karanga people.

Cave paintings

Hillside Dam—6 kms from the town centre off the Hillside Rd. Small, pretty lake, surrounded by nature reserve and bird sanctuary. Also has an aloe garden worth seeing.

Mabukuwene Park, 12 hectares in size, 10 km from the city centre, with aloe garden, bird sanctury, a wide variety of indigenous trees and good view over the city. Take the Hillside Road and on into Burnside Rd, then turn right into Chipping Way and you will reach the gates after a kilometre.

Intricately patterned ancient wall

Naletale Ruins. Follow the Harare Road for 96 km, as far as Daisyfield, then turn right and go another 24 km. The ruins are about a kilometre's walk from the road on top of a small kopje. The structure, which is just one oval wall about 45 metres in diameter, uses chevron, herringbone, cord and chequer patterning as well as lines of dark stones and coloured stone insects to create the most highly decorated dry stone walling yet found in the country. It is of a late period and seems to have been left unfinished.

Site of the royal kraal

State House and the Indaba Tree, 6 km north of Bulawayo, branching off the Victoria Falls Road. Now, sadly, closed to the public, this is the site of Lobengula's royal kraal from 1881 onwards. Destroyed in 1896, the only reminder of his presence is the Indaba Tree, an old and none too healthy tree in whose shade he was said to hold his council meetings and negotiations. State House was built shortly after Lobengula's flight when Bulawayo became the British South Africa Company's Matabele headquarters. Also in the grounds is a rondaavel built for Rhodes during one of his visits to the city which now houses a photographic display, and some mock-Tudor stables that have been preserved as a National Monument, with elaborate cast iron work imported from Scotland.

Tshabalala Sanctuary, 8 km from Bulawayo along the Matopos Road. A small game park run by the National Parks Service, it contains a wide variety of small game but none of the large predators or 'giants'. Walking is permitted through the sanctuary. Open from 6am to 6pm.

KHAMI RUINS

**Rivalling Great
Zimbabwe**

Second in importance only to Great Zimbabwe, the
Khami Ruins are smaller but still cover a vast,
sprawling area and are impressive, a mass of complex dry stone terracing and walls that can give
a truer sense of the community than Great Zimbabwe's more scattered settlements. In many ways
I prefer Khami's magnificient rocky setting and
peaceful blend of history and landscape.

Getting There

The ruins lie 22 km west of Bulawayo. Take 11th
Avenue westwards and follow it as it turns into
the Khami Road. The turning into the site is on
the right just after the Khami River Bridge. There
are a couple of car parks near the ruins. Wear comfortable shoes if you want to explore properly and
be prepared for a lot of walking, some fairly
arduous.

History

The original name of the site is not known, though
there are several possibilities. Local tribesmen call
the ruins Zimbabgwi, which is a dialectic variation
on Zimbabwe or 'houses of stone'. The Ndebele
call them talanga or 'walls' and the Karanga 'the
place of Madhladhla' who was the last of the mambos (priest-kings) to rule here. Even the origin of
the word Khami is disputed. Lobengula's family
name was Khumalo, the name of the river on early
maps. Some say however that it could also be the
Sesotho word for 'slow flowing', while others claim
it was named for Khama, an early ruler of nearby
Botswana.

**Lobengula's
secret**

Though white men were visiting Matabeleland
regularly from the 1850s, nothing was known of
the site at Khami until Lobengula's death in 1893.
It is thought that the king still used the site, perhaps
for rainmaking ceremonies, and the whole area was

designated a King's Preserve, shielded from prying eyes. The first explorations of the site, starting in 1895, were unabashed treasure hunting under the control of the Rhodesia Ancient Ruins Company Limited. The company was dissolved in 1900 and shortly afterwards a long series of more scientific investigations led to bitter battles over the origin and date of the complex. These continued intermittently for several decades until the last excavations in the 1950s resulted in the publication of a 'definitive' study in 1959. No work has been done on the site since.

One hundred thousand years of settlement

Artefacts found at the site suggest that there has been almost continuous human occupation here for about 100,000 years. The first evidence of the use of iron can be dated to 1800 years ago. The builders of the visible ruins—the stone terraces and walls—were part of the Rozwi culture which reached its zenith from the 15th to 17th C AD and here, as at Great Zimbabwe, there is evidence of worldwide trade links, with a good smattering of Portuguese, German and Chinese pottery. Although no major new building seems to have been done after about AD 1700, the Rozwi continued to live here, the later phases providing evidence of trade with Europe such as paraffin tins, Victorian china and iron cooking pots.

Homes of the aristocracy

The walls seem to have been built primarily as symbols of prestige rather than as fortifications and as the terraces hold a relatively small number of dwellings these monumental works were probably the homes of the aristocracy while the majority of the people lived in huts scattered over the nearby slopes. The site was abandoned with the advent of the Ndebele in about 1830 and a legend that blames the Zulu impis (a body of warriors) for its destruction is probably rooted in fact.

Looking Around Khami

Start at the small site museum near the car park which gives a rapid roundup of the history of the site as well as showing a selection of the artefacts found here.

There are 12 main ruins spread over a wide area surrounded by smaller outbuildings and huts. The **Hill Ruin**, the highest point in the area, is the most important complex and has excellent views. On top are three large terraces, built with earth and gravel brought up from the valley below and held by dry stone walling. Within this complex are the remains of some hut floors and nearby is a narrow passageway, originally thought to have had a pole and daga roof. The scorch marks of the fire that destroyed the site are still visible along the passage walls. It has been suggested that this was a secret passage leading to the quarters of the priest or witchdoctor.

The high point

Next comes the **Cross Ruin**, still an enigma. The cross, that of the Dominican Order, was thought to have been laid out by visiting missionaries in the 16th or 17th C. The **Vlei Ruins** are reached by a footpath several hundred metres long and consist of a terraced platform and the remains of three huts. The interior walls and drains are thought to be cattle kraals. Another footpath leads to the **Precipice Ruin** near the reservoir, a massive retaining wall 68 metres long and over 6 metres high, some of which is submerged when the dam is full.

Family dwelling

From here you can walk round the lake and up another footpath to the **Passage Ruin**, a roughly circular enclosure entered by a passage 18 metres long. This seems to have been a family home with both living quarters and stock enclosures. The Passage and Precipice Ruins are both accessible from another car park should you not wish to walk quite so far. There is a picnic site on the far side of the lake.

MATOBO NATIONAL PARK

Extraordinary landscape

One of Zimbabwe's great natural wonders, the Matopos Hills cover an area of almost 2000 sq km, much of it a sweeping sea of granite 3000 million years old, stripped bare by erosion, twisted into sculpture by the wind and coloured red and gold by lichens. Mzilikazi was the one to call the hills Matobo or 'bald-headed ones', a name later corrupted by the white settlers to Matopos. Rhodes too was so impressed by the area that at his request 43,200 hectares (432 sq km) were turned into a National Park. And it was here that he asked to be buried.

It is possible to see all the sites of the Matopos in a single day, but if possible it is worth spending longer, allowing yourself plenty of time to unwind and walk or just to sit and watch the light play over the rocks and rippling sheets of grass. Fishing and pony trekking are also possible and there is a small game park.

Entering the Park

The entrance to the park is about 30 km from Bulawayo along the Matopos Road (a continuation of Robert Mugabe Way). Walking, cycling, etc, are possible in all parts of the park other than the game reserve.

Rhodes' houses

About one kilometre before you reach the entrance to the park you will see on the right-hand side of the road a palatial white building. Now a prep school, it was **Rhodes' Matabeleland home**. A short distance further and there is a turn-off to the right leading up to **Rhodes' summer house**, a small open-sided building with magnificent views out over the valleys. It was here that his body rested while his grave was prepared in the hills. In the valley below you can see the orderly fields of Zimbabwe's foremost agricultural research station.

The main road through the park does a loop.

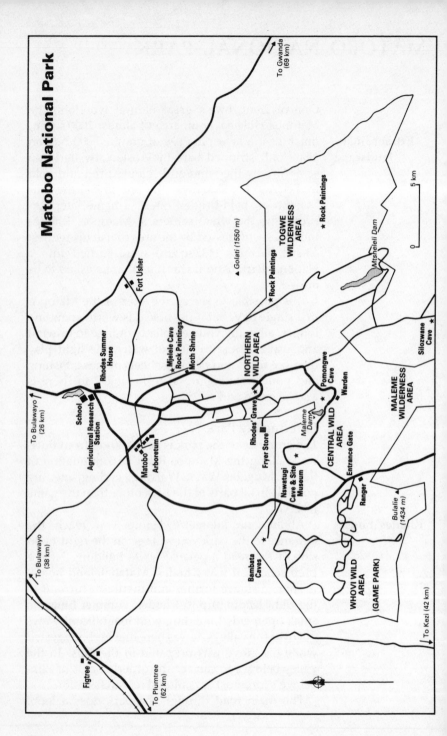

Matobo National Park

To Gwanda (69 km)

Fort Usher

▲ Golati (1550 m)

Rhodes Summer House

Mjelele Cave
★ Rock Paintings
Moth Shrine

TOGWE WILDERNESS AREA

★ Rock Paintings

★ Rock Paintings

Mtsheleli Dam

0   5 km

To Bulawayo (26 km)

School

Agricultural Research Station

Matobo Arboretum

NORTHERN WILD AREA

Rhodes' Grave
Fryer Store

Maleme Dam

Pomongwe Cave
Warden

MALEME WILDERNESS AREA

Silozwane Cave ★

To Bulawayo (38 km)

Nswatugi Cave & Site Museum

CENTRAL WILD AREA

Entrance Gate

Ranger

▲ Bulalie (1434 m)

Bembata Caves

WHOVI WILD AREA (GAME PARK)

To Kezi (42 km)

Figtree

To Plumtree (62 km)

Cave painting of a cheetah hunt in Matobo National Park

You are quite likely to see small game such as antelope, monkeys or dassies (rock rabbits), so keep your eyes open. There are also many species of lizard and snakes. The snakes shouldn't bother you, but watch where you put your hands if climbing rocks.

Towards the View of the World
Off the road on the left are the **Mjelele Cave Rock Paintings**. These are the first but by no means the best of the cave paintings that can be seen throughout the area, many of them dating back thousands of years. They were mainly painted by the original Bushmen inhabitants, though some of the latest, clumsiest work is thought to have been copy-cat art by later Bantu invaders. Most of the paintings

are now in very poor condition, the constant traffic of sightseers and cameras fading the natural paints. An exact but clearer replica of some of the Matobo paintings can be seen in the Bulawayo Natural History Museum. The earliest of the surviving paintings are abstract hand prints or simple patterning. Later come naturalistic representations of local animals followed shortly by more complex scenes of native life, in particular the hunt.

Evolution of cave painting

Virtually next door to the cave is the grandiose **Moth Shrine** to the dead of the wars, erected by members of the Memorable Order of Tin Hats. The White Rhino Shelter, decorated by the Bushmen, is on the left-hand side of the road.

You soon come to the **View of the World**, a massive granite dome at the high point of the hills, its sweeping curves dominating the whole area. To the locals it is sacred; they call it Malindidzimu, 'the place of spirits'. It was Rhodes who called it the 'View of the World' and it was here that he asked to be buried.

Rhodes' grave

That Rhodes was a brilliant man cannot be disputed, though many of his activities might not be in line with modern thought. Fifth son of an English country clergyman, he was a millionaire and Member of the Cape Parliament by the age of 27 and Prime Minister of the Cape by the age of 37, by which time he also controlled almost all of South Africa's diamond industry. He was responsible for Britain's colonisation of Botswana, Zimbabwe, Zambia and Malawi, was head of the British South Africa Company, and was the moving force behind the building of most of southern Africa's railways. In his first will he wanted to leave his fortune for the creation of secret society to ensure Britain's domination of the entire world. This was changed, but a lasting benefit was the provision in the final draft of funds for a number of scholarships for Commonwealth students to study at Oxford. Today, to be a Rhodes scholar is one of the highest accolades of scholastic achievement. He died in Cape Town in 1902 and his body was transported by train to

Rhodes scholarships

Bulawayo, then by ox cart to the Matopos where a grave had to be blasted into the granite.

Also atop the granite dome is the **grave of Leander Starr Jameson**, Rhodes' right-hand man and famous as leader of the Jameson Raid (the 1895 rebellion against President Kruger of South Africa) and the **grave of Sir Charles Coghlan** who became first prime minister of Rhodesia after the 1923 elections. There is also a **Memorial to the Shangaan Patrol**. On 3 December 1893, during the Matabele Wars, a patrol of 20 men, headed by Allan Wilson, was sent to check out a rumour that the fleeing Lobengula was in the area. The patrol met a bunch of 'demoralised Matabele warriors' and followed them into the forest, not realising that it was being **Zulu ambush** led into an ambush carefully planned by Mtjaan, one of the King's generals. A message sent back to headquarters asking for a maxim gun was ignored, though reinforcements were sent. Early the next morning, the group, now numbering 34, moved out to find themselves facing an impi of 30,000 Zulu warriors. By dusk the entire patrol and 400 Zulus were dead. The Zulus honoured their bravery, calling them 'men of men'. They were all buried where they had died but on 5 July 1904 were moved to the Matopos where the Shangaan memorial was unveiled.

Further into the Park

8 km south of View of the World is another set of Bushmen cave paintings in **Pomongwe Cave** near the Maleme dam. A further 5 km to the northwest is **Nswatugi Cave**. Nswatugi is a Karanga word meaning 'the place of jumping'. Legend has it that the Karanga god, Mlimo, once jumped from his dwelling place at Njelele, 40 km away, over the top of Nswatugi Hill, touching its top with one foot as he passed and finally landing at Kalanyoni, some **Best preserved** distance further. The paintings here, which are per- **paintings** haps the best preserved of all those on view in the Matopos, are up a steep rocky staircase. There is a tiny museum by the car park which gives a little

background to the Matobo paintings and a detailed map of the area.

The western sector of Matobo has been fenced off as a reserve for small game. This is **Whovi Wild Area**, where most animals except elephants and the big cats can be seen. Normal game park regulations apply.

Accommodation

There are no hotels or restaurants within the National Park, but there are several **Camping and caravan sites**. Take all supplies, including food and fuel as there are no stores or garages.

Maleme Dam, south of View of the World, is the main camp with a selection of small chalets and lodges as well as a camping and caravan site. It is a pretty site, right beside a lake, but the approach is steep and can be difficult with a caravan.

There are also camping and caravan sites with ablution blocks and hot and cold water at *Mtshelele Dam* in the southeast of the park and at the *Arboretum*, near the north entrance.

Information from and bookings through the National Parks Central Reservations Office, Harare. Post Bag K5142, Bulawayo. Tel: Matopos 0-1913.

MASVINGO AND ENVIRONS

Struggling to save the veld from erosion

The southern low veld is the agricultural heartland of Zimbabwe, its rich red dust heavily irrigated to feed the intensive plantations of maize, sugar and cotton. It is here that farming reaches its most hi-tech, but it is also in this area that much of the land was nearly destroyed by over-grazing and over-population in the old Tribal Trust Lands, cattle spreading out to close-crop the brown grass of the acacia scrubland, goats fighting over the last few clumps struggling for survival near the villages. Much of the area has been returned to the bush since independence in a last-ditch effort to halt the erosion that was slowly but surely turning the area to a desert wasteland, and the villagers have been moved to more fertile ground to set up co-ops with careful overseeing by agricultural experts.

The Market Town of Masvingo

Masvingo is a small place, with a population of about 40,000 and mainly acts as an agricultural market town for the southern low veld. The surrounding area has also become one of Zimbabwe's main tourist destinations. Fort Victoria, as Masvingo was until recently called, was the first of the towns created by the pioneer column in August 1890. The first fort was actually a few kilometres away but due to a shortage of water the whole settlement was moved in July 1892 to its present position.

The Masvingo and District Publicity Association is on Robert Mugabe Street (opposite the Chevron Hotel). PO Box 340, Masvingo. Tel: 2643.

Getting There and Around

There are good **roads** from all the main centres in Zimbabwe (although a stretch of the route between Masvingo and Mutare still leaves something to be desired) and from the Beit Bridge border post with South Africa.

A scheduled **air service** from Harare and Gweru

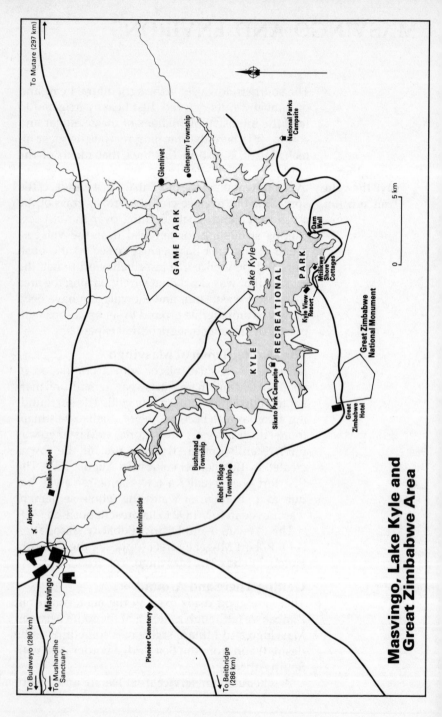

Masvingo, Lake Kyle and Great Zimbabwe Area

runs five days a week. Organise transport from the airport before arriving as UTC only runs tours to Great Zimbabwe a couple of times a week and these are the only days on which the plane is met.

There are daily **coaches** from Bulawayo and two or three a week from Harare.

There are **guided tours** to Great Zimbabwe and Kyle dam wall from Masvingo. A **local bus** service to Morgenster Mission, which goes close to the ruins, operates three times a day from the Mucheke Bus Terminal, Charumbira Street. Ask the Publicity Association for details of times.

Car hire is by Hertz which operates through a local travel agency. They will arrange for your car to meet you at the airport if required. Travelworld, Founders House, Robert Mugabe Street. PO Box 658, Masvingo. Tel: 2131. Telex: 3499.

Things to See in and near Town
The original **Fort** and **pioneer cemetery** are just a few kilometres out along the Beit Bridge Road.

Italian Church. A large number of Italian prisoners of war were confined in camps in Rhodesia during the Second World War, many of them electing to stay on afterwards. The chapel dedicated to St Francis was built by the prisoners from 1942 to 46, the paintings and mosaics in the apse being done by one of them, a civil engineer. Between 1956 and 1957 the two wings were added by the Italian authorities who also decorated the aisles and built the tombs for the 71 men who had died in the camps. The church is 5 km from Masvingo on the left side of the Mutare Road.

Accommodation in Town
There are no upmarket or really cheap **hotels** within Masvingo or the surrounding area—only middle range to budget ones. Stay out of town if possible. The standards are much higher for much the same price.

Chevron**, Robert Mugabe Street, Masvingo. PO Box 245. Tel: 2054/5.

Flamboyant Motel**, 1.5 km from town on the Beit Bridge Road. PO Box 225. Tel: 2006/5.

Municipal **camping and caravan site** one kilometre from the town centre on the Mutare Road. Large and rather boring, but it has full facilities and is pleasant enough. PO Box 17, Masvingo. Tel: 2431 ext. 60.

Sightseeing in the Surrounding Area

Morgenster Mission. Two natural monoliths, the 'Finger Rocks', guard the entrance to the mission, about 35 km from Masvingo past Great Zimbabwe. There is also a panoramic view—'World's View' of course—that is one of the finest in Zimbabwe. The mission runs a school for the deaf.

One of Zimbabwe's finest panoramas

Mushandike Sanctuary, 27 km west of Masvingo along the Mashava Road. This is a small dam and a wildlife sanctuary where most of the animals have been reintroduced. There is a wide variety of antelope, wildebeeste, etc, as well as birds, but few big game species. Several species of fish are found at the dam and fishing permits are obtainable from the park warden. There is a small and fairly basic camping and caravan site. Bookings to the Warden, Post Bag 9036, Masvingo. Tel: Mashava 24412.

Serina Mission Church. 20 kms from Masvingo on the Mvuma Rd. An extraordinary monument begun in 1948 and built and decorated by mission pupils. A cross between English Catholic and Zimbabwean tribal art.

KYLE

Kyle Dam, the second largest in Zimbabwe, was built across the Mtilikwe River to irrigate the rich agricultural lands of Victoria Province. Completed in 1961, it is 60 metres high and 305 metres across. When full, the **lake** covers 90 sq km, with an incredibly beautiful, ragged and rocky shoreline. An area of 18,000 hectares that includes the lake and much of the shore has been declared a National Park.

Enjoying the Fauna, Flora and Views

To reach the dam wall, take the road from Masvingo to Great Zimbabwe and follow it on for about a further 15 km. The last section of this road, which continues on over the dam wall as Murray McDou-

Kyle Lake and Dam, an attractive recreation area

gall Drive, hugs the lake shore for much of the way and has many spectacular views. The Mtilikwe Gorge is made from great slabs of barren granite, with a few aloes and cacti growing wild from the crevices. Keep an eye open for leguaans or water monitors which are prolific in the area. These are **Africa's largest** Africa's largest lizards, growing up to 2.5 metres **lizards** long, although to see one that size is rare. Their size alone makes them unmistakable, but note that the young are black with yellow stripes on the head, rows of yellow spots on the back and orange bands on the tail, while the adults are normally a murky olive with faint yellowy markings. They move fast, use their tails for defence and can have a nasty bite.

There is fishing and boating on the lake. Boats can be hired from the Kyle View Chalets on the south shore.

Kyle Game Park

About 7600 hectares of land on the north shore of the lake has been fenced off as a game park with 64 km of dirt roads laid out for game viewing. Most of the animals were introduced to the area but are now breeding happily, including a small colony of **White rhinos** white rhinos. There are no elephants or big predators, but the park is one of the most attractive in the country and you will normally see a good variety of game. Game viewing on horse-back is a major attraction here, enabling you to get off the roads and closer to the animals. The entrance to the park is about 35 km from Masvingo, with a turning to the right off the Mutare Road about 15 km from town.

Accommodation Around the Lake

Glenlivet Hotel: 45 km from Masvingo off the Mutare Road, this small hotel is in a very pretty area along the north shore (though not on the shore itself) of the lake. It will arrange boats and fishing. PO Box 146, Masvingo. Tel: 7611.

Kyle View Holiday Resort: On the southern shore of

the lake, 6 km from Great Zimbabwe. Reasonably priced, with a selection of fully furnished chalets and a camping and caravan site. It also has a swimming pool, bar, restaurant and store. Boats available for hire. Post Bag 9055, Masvingo. Tel: 223822.

Mtilikwe Lake Shore Lodges: Also on the south shore, a little further along towards the dam wall. A selection of fully furnished lodges and a caravan and camping site. Prettier than Kyle View, but no bar or food. Reasonable prices. PO Box 518, Masvingo. Tel: 292421.

Sikato Bay Camp: On a peninsula on the west shore of the lake, about 6 km from Great Zimbabwe. Caravan and camping site with ablution blocks, but no other facilities. Run by National Parks Service. Post Bag 9136, Masvingo. Tel: 223820.

Accommodation within Kyle Game Park

There is a small rest camp with fully furnished one- and two-bedroom lodges and a caravan and camping site within the park by *Chenyati Bay* on the north side of the lake. The camp site is basic but it is probably my favourite in the whole country, built on a rocky peninsula that stretches down to the lake shore. I've never seen it full, and the view, especially at sunrise and sunset, is quite magnificent. Post Bag 9136, Masvingo. Tel: 2913. Bookings for National Parks sites through their Central Bookings Office, Harare (see Appendix).

GREAT ZIMBABWE

Second only to the Pyramids

The largest stone structure in Africa after the Pyramids, Great Zimbabwe has been the centre of an empire, the inspiration of legend and the symbol of freedom, giving its name to a country. It is by far the most important of Zimbabwe's historical monuments and the only one that has been thoroughly researched. It is an odd site, both inspiring and disappointing; inspiring because of its monumental size, disappointing because it is difficult to understand without a great deal of effort. The type of building here is completely at odds with the European norm and the unexplained enclosures can easily look like heaps of old stone. Heresy perhaps to say this, but I do so only to suggest you take the time to sort out some of the seemingly purposeless walls.

Getting There

It is 28 km from Masvingo to Great Zimbabwe, south of Lake Kyle. For those without cars there are organised tours several times a week and the local bus to Morgenster Mission goes to within walking distance of the site.

Accommodation

*Great Zimbabwe Hotel***: A small, rambling hotel within easy walking distance of the ruins. This is mid-range pricewise, very pleasant and the best hotel in the Masvingo district. Post Bag 9082, Masvingo. Tel: 2274/2449. Or book through Zimbabwe Sun Central Bookings Office, Harare (see Appendix).

History

There are two possible origins of the word zimbabwe, both in the Shona language. The first is dzimba dza mabwe or 'houses of stone', the second dzimba woye or 'venerated houses'. Whichever it

The mysterious cone within the Great Enclosure

is, it is a name that has always been given to royal residences, chiefs' houses and graves. There are 150 known zimbabwes in the country.

The first excavations at Great Zimbabwe began in 1902; they were followed by others at intermittent intervals and still continue today. Most of the

**Distortion
by white
governments
of Great
Zimbabwe's
true
significance**

site has been explored by now, much of it unfortunately using crude techniques that have destroyed as much as they discovered. Great Zimbabwe has also been a political football, with the white government insisting that the blacks could not build anything so sophisticated and setting out in all their research to prove it. Some said it was Arab, some Phoenician, some even that it was Egyptian. And the large amounts of restoration carried out over the decades all sought to prove the point, borrowing stylistically from all these sources. Since independence, things have swung almost too far in the other direction, with too little influence from the outside being allowed in spite of the obviously great trade links with the coast.

The earliest signs of man's presence on the site date back to the Gokomere people of about AD 300, though there is no surviving record of any settled community living here at that time. It is not until

Zimbabwe birds, symbol of a nation

the 11th C that the town appears to have become established, part of a fragmented society that had taken to living in small groups in the hills. The first use of stone came over a century later at the beginning of the 13th C, and within another 100 years the city-state was flourishing, a sophisticated complex of buildings that housed over 10,000 people at its height. Archaeological finds show that it was a religious and temporal capital of great wealth and influence.

Flourishing city-state

But by the late 15th C it was already in decline as the centralised empire split up and the Mwene Mutapa's capital moved to Fura Mountain. Zimbabwe never again had the same power but remained a royal city, ruled over by the NeManwa dynasty until the late 18th C when it was deposed by a Karanga ruler called Mugabe! His dynasty ruled until 1834 when Zwangendaba, a rival of Shaka's, and his followers the Ngoni, attacked the town, massacring its inhabitants and throwing the last of the mambos to his death from a hill since known as Thaba Zi Ka Mambo.

At its heyday the city was a lively one, with evidence of gold and other metal working, a rich trade with the coast that brought in such luxuries as Chinese porcelain, a large textile industry and a massive dependency on cattle for food and wealth.

Looking Around the Site

Start at the small **museum** which gives a good if basic background to the site as well as displaying a variety of finds including the famous Zimbabwe birds. Seven complete birds and half of another have been found at Zimbabwe, most of them on the Hill where they had been placed on pillars a metre high. They are thought to have been a family totem or crest, possibly memorials to dead ancestors. They are all about 40 cm tall and are carved from a greeny-grey soapstone. Although obviously birds, they are not very realistic, crouching on legs more like a mammal's leading one archaeologist

The Zimbabwe bird

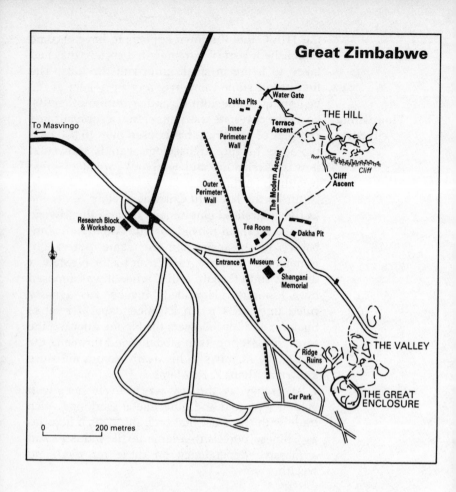

Great Zimbabwe

To Masvingo

Dakha Pits

Water Gate

THE HILL

Inner Perimeter Wall

Terrace Ascent

The Modern Ascent

Cliff

Cliff Ascent

Outer Perimeter Wall

Research Block & Workshop

Tea Room

Dakha Pit

Entrance

Museum

Shangani Memorial

THE VALLEY

Ridge Ruins

Car Park

THE GREAT ENCLOSURE

0   200 metres

at least to suggest that they are 'supernatural composite creatures of mythology'. They have been symbolic to both white Rhodesia and black Zimbabwe, appearing on stamps, in the country's crest and on its currency. Several of them were taken to Cape Town at the end of the last century and were returned only in 1985. Even that caused controversy as they were swapped for a collection of butterflies from the Bulawayo Museum, one of the finest collections of its kind in the world, leaving local butterfly lovers up in arms.

A number of large, flat soapstone dishes have

also been found as well as a variety of small soapstone and pottery figurines from early periods that are thought possibly to have been votive offerings. One enclosure in the valley was discovered in 1902 to contain the royal treasury which included vast numbers of iron hoes, many of them unused, and probably given as tribute. Iron was rare and vastly expensive—a single hoe was enough to buy a bride. There was also a great deal of iron, copper and bronze wire, thousands of Indian glass beads, Chinese dishes and iron gongs and spearheads.

Votive offerings and tribute

The **Great Enclosure** is largest and most important of all the buildings at Zimbabwe. It is also known by its 19th C Karanga name of Imba huru or 'Great House'. The *outer wall* is a massive feat of masonry, 255 metres round, constructed from a million granite blocks with a total estimated weight of 15,000 tonnes. It was begun in the northwest segment; techniques improved dramatically as it worked its way round in an anti-clockwise direction to the northeast. At this end it is 11 metres high, 6 metres thick at the base and 4 metres thick at the top.

A massive feat of masonry

The *narrow passage* leading round the interior of the enclosure is in fact formed by the original outer wall. By the time the circle had been completed, the building was so superior to this original wall that they started round again rather than trying to improve what was already there. The smaller, earlier wall was left inside. On the southeast segment round the outside is a *ring of chevron patterning*.

The *interior of the enclosure* is a mass of smaller enclosures, old hut floors, animal enclosures and platforms that seem to have had some ceremonial use, one at least possibly being a sacrificial altar. There is also one area which shows evidence of metal working. It is thought that the enclosure was the home of the royal family from about the mid-13th C, with five or six households living here.

The enigma of the tower

The *conical tower* in the southeast segment is probably Zimbabwe's most famous—and enigmatic—monument. It is a late addition and stands 10

187

Fortifications on The Hill, Great Zimbabwe's earliest settlement site

metres high, is 5 metres in diameter at the base and is 2 metres in diameter at the top. It is solid right through. The tower used to have three rings of dentelle patterning round its top, but no one knows what the original shape of the top was. The experts agree that it is a ritual symbol of some sort, but some say it is phallic, some that it represents the male authority of the king and some that it is the shape of a grain store and thus represents the ruler's generosity in sharing out his tribute.

Leaving the Great Enclosure by the north entrance, a pathway leads among a granite **ridge** covered by a variety of small enclosures and terraces that seem to have been more short-lived housing for smaller groups. Many of the walls here were of poorer construction, thought to be the 18th C work of the Karanga invaders. As the path divides at the end of the ridge you will see a bare irregular circle that was once the **Royal Treasury**. The finds from here are now in the site museum.

Down in the **valley** is a jumbled collection of smaller properties, many of them with extremely sophisticated stone walling and terracing. To the north of this main complex is a series of **six grand entrances** probably marking the entrance to the aristocratic quarter. The commoners lived cheek by jowl in a crowded area between here and the south face of the hill.

The **Hill Enclosure** was the first area of the site to be inhabited, the Western Enclosure showing signs of continuous occupation for over 300 years. Originally the royal home, in later years it became the province of the priests. There are now two paths leading to the summit, the first using an old route for much of the way, with steep, narrow, uneven steps not suitable for anyone but the fit. The second, modern path curls round the site of the hill in a gentler curve. Both lead into the *Western Enclosure* by what is thought to have been a smaller private entrance to the living area. As each dakha hut collapsed it was spread out to provide the base of the next, with new clay, dug at the base of the hill, being brought up for the next building. This has left, in those parts not touched by earlier investigators, an exceptionally good stratigraphy that has provided the basis of dating for the site. The wall of the Western Enclosure is massive, 8 metres high and 5 metres thick, and had a line of turrets and pillars all the way round at 2-metre intervals. The few that are now evident were reconstructed in 1916 when the wall itself was rebuilt.

From here, the only original doorway at Zimbabwe leads through a covered passage into a series of smaller enclosures, which are thought to be the private quarters of the priest or spirit medium. A network of small passages criss-crosses the hill, providing private access to many areas.

The *Eastern Enclosure* seems to have been the public entrance, with a more grandiose gateway. When it was first discovered, this enclosure contained

The earliest inhabited area

several highly decorated dakha platforms, topped by dozens of stone pillars, six of them with Zimbabwe birds on top. Many other dishes and smaller figurines were also found in this area.

GONAREZHOU NATIONAL PARK

Gonarezhou is one of the most distant and least developed of Zimbabwe's national parks—which means it is extremely isolated indeed. It covers some 5000 km on the Mozambique border in the southwest of the country, in an area that was a major battleground during the war and has also been one of the main haunts of ivory poachers.

Bad-tempered elephants It has a high elephant population (its name means Place of the Elephants) but the history of the area has left them bad-tempered and extremely wary, so they can be dangerous. In all, the animals here are less used to humans and haven't had good experiences with those they have encountered, so will be shyer than on the more commonly trodden tourist trail.

There are some tracks within the path that are negotiable in an ordinary saloon car, but as these are few try and get hold of a four-wheel-drive. No motorbikes or boats are allowed in, and there is no source of food or fuel closer than Chiredzi, so you must take in adequate supplies. The park is open only from May to October.

Gonarezhou is split into two sections, each administered separately.

Malabauta Area
This is about 2500 sq km in area and stretches from the Mozambique border to the Mwenezi River in the south. To get there take the Tanganda Road from Chiredzi for about 20 km. Turn right past Chipinda Pools, over the Lundi River and follow the signs to Malabauta/Swimuwini Camps. It is about 159 km from Chiredzi. If coming from South Africa, there is an alternative route via Rutenga and Boli.

Accommodation
Swimuwini (the Place of Baobabs) Rest Camp: 8 km from the Warden's Office on the Mwenezi River. There

are five small chalets with basic furniture and central ablution facilities.

Malabauta: There is a small caravan and camping site about 600 metres from the Warden's Office with full facilities, although no luxuries.

Address for both: Post Bag 7017, Chiredzi. Bookings through National Parks Central Bookings Office, Harare.

Chipinda Pools

Two further sub-sections, Lundi and Sabi, are administered from here. The entry point to the park is off the Tanganda Road from Chiredzi. Chipinda Pools is 59 km from Chiredzi, on the north bank of the Lundi River.

Accommodation

There are no chalets in this region, only a few very basic, usually very isolated camp sites. Only those at *Chipinda Pools* and *Chinguli* have ablution blocks and caravans can only be taken to Chipinda Pools. There are seven other, undeveloped, campsites for individual groups of up to ten people which will be allocated when you book. Fishing is permitted on the Lundi River only, and only from within the confines of the camp. Post Bag 7003, Chiredzi. Bookings through the National Parks Central Booking Office, Harare.

SECTION 5:
THE EASTERN
HIGHLANDS

Mutare

The Vumba

The Nyanga

The Chimanimani

TO MUTARE

Another Africa

Manicaland, Zimbabwe's eastern province, is in every way a contrast to the dry savannah bush that typifies so much of the country—and so much of the rest of Africa. For about 500 km along the Mozambique border runs a series of mountain chains, each as different from the next as they are from the rest of the country. This is the land of pine forests and lakes, trout fishing and orchards, craggy cliffs and open moorland. It is an area that rings with memories of 'home', and its names—Troutbeck and Connemara—echo the nostalgia it created in the settlers. It is not in any way the 'true Africa' the European tourist is usually looking for, but it is where many of the Zimbabweans themselves go on holiday, looking for an escape from the burning summer sun. It also provides the best hiking in the country.

It is best to have your own transport here. There is no scheduled air service, though there are some private airfields; there is one train and one coach to Mutare each day from Harare; and within the area there are intermittent local buses but nothing at all to take you to the places most worth visiting. Hitching is possible, but time-consuming, and the steep hills make cycling impractical for all but the most fit.

The land is high and the climate very different from the rest of the country, generally 5 to 10°C cooler than elsewhere, although Mutare's sheltered position can lead to very hot, humid weather in summer. In the winter the weather is often grey, misty and drizzly—known locally as guti—and the summer electric storms bounce off the mountains to become more spectacular and ferocious than ever. Winter nights can go down to freezing, log fires blaze and heavy jumpers are needed out of doors. Even so, the weather will still be a delight for most northern Europeans, and I have sun-

194

bathed on mid-winter's day.

War damage Manicaland was the region probably worst hit by the war of 1970s, the long border and remote hills providing excellent cover for the guerrilla troops. It is only now beginning to recover from the damage that turned it into a no-go area for years. Some hotels are still closed, and right on the border the minefields lie hidden, waiting for an incautious move to show their presence.

Mutare

Set in a bowl in the hills, Mutare is the prettiest of Zimbabwe's main towns, its low white buildings stretched along broad streets lined with the brilliant purple and red of jacarandahs and flame trees. It has a population of nearly 200,000 and is Zim-
Time warp babwe's third city yet the centre, at least, feels more like a ghost town, the streets almost empty of people, the shops and even the background musak unchanged over the ten years since I had left. More than in any other part of the country, I felt, walking down Main Street, as though I'd stepped into a time warp.

The city has had two main functions in its life—as a centre for the Eastern Highlands and the local farming community, which still continues; and as a frontier post on the popular route to the Mozambique coast, a border rarely crossed these days except by troops. Mutare has become isolated from the mainstream of even Zimbabwean society, and as there are no major tourist attractions nearby, few overseas visitors get this far.

History

Mutare has moved several times in its brief life, starting off a few kilometres further north, near the village of Penhalonga where the Chikanga—the local chief—had his court. Around it the first few white settlers, gold prospectors to a man, built a tiny, straggling community in the 1880s. On the arrival of the British South Africa Company in 1891 a new site was chosen for the town, 16 km north

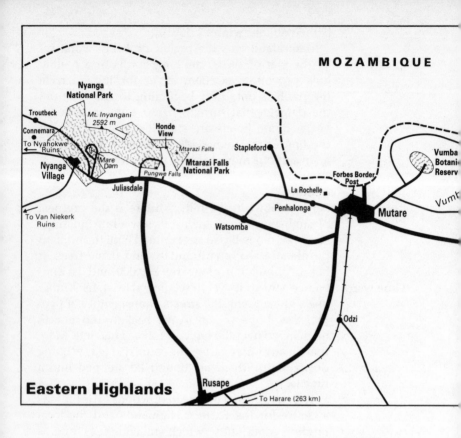

of the present one, along the Umtali river. There is still a small village there, now known as Old Umtali.

If the railway can't go to Umtali, Umtali will go to the railway

The town's final move came in 1896 when it was realised that the lie of the land would make it impossible to route the new railway from Beira through Umtali if it was to be continued on to Salisbury. The area was surveyed and the whole town moved, lock, stock and barrel to its present position. The railway reached the town in February 1898 and the Salisbury connection was completed in 1899.

Umtali's name was changed to Mutare after independence in 1980.

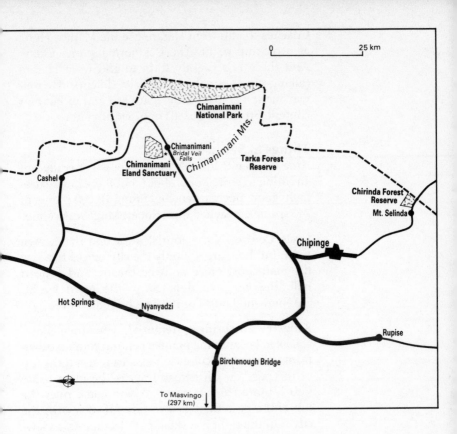

The Mutare and District Publicity Association Office is on Market Square, on the corner of Robert Mugabe Avenue and Herbert Chitepo Street. PO Box 69, Mutare. Tel: 64711.

Getting Around

Car hire can be arranged through the tourist office. There are a few **taxis** (tel: 63344) but they are significantly more expensive than in Harare.

Local buses to outlying rural areas are based at the market place in Sakubva, the high density suburb out on the road towards Masvingo. These are intermittent and there is nothing to speak of at all within the town.

Coaches to and from Harare use the Manica Hotel as a pick-up point. There is normally one a day. And there is a nightly **train** to and from Harare (taking nine hours to do the 260-odd km). The railway station is just off the southern end of Herbert Chitepo Street. Tel: 62801 or 62896 after hours.

Things to See in Mutare

Aloe Garden. Mutare's main park is generally not anything to write home about, but there is an extremely good aloe garden containing 10,000 plants of 243 species. Reached from Robert Mugabe Avenue.

Civic Centre. Not a tourist attraction in its own right, but here are not only the city offices but also the main post office and the theatre and concert hall, the last two donated to the town by Sir Stephen and Lady Courtauld who retired here.

Kingsley Fairbridge Memorial. Christmas Pass, so-called because the pioneer column coming down from Salisbury to colonise this area reached the top of the pass on Christmas Day, is the main route into Mutare from Harare. As you come over the top of the pass there is a wonderful view over the city. On the right is a small path leading to a viewing point called Chace's View. On the left is a road leading up to the Kingsley Fairbridge Memorial. Fairbridge was a poet and educationalist, a Rhodes scholar who himself established the Fairbridge Scholarships to the Universities of Salisbury and Perth, founding too a number of farm training schools in Australia, Canada and Rhodesia. It is a pleasant place for a walk and again has an excellent view. It is the traditional place to view the sunrise after a night out on the town.

Cecil Kop Nature Reserve. The road to the Kingsley Fairbridge Memorial continues on up the hill for about 3.5 km to Mutare Heights, where the view gets better than ever and there is good walking in a reserved wilderness area, part of the Nature Reserve set up and run by the Wildlife Society of

Zimbabwe. The road is solid hairpins and very poor. In the rainy season you should only try it in a four-wheel drive vehicle.

Game park. At the other end of this ridge is a small game park, reached from Arcadia Avenue or Circular Drive. There is a viewing platform at Tiger's Kloof Dam, but elsewhere in the game park you must stay in your car. The park area is very small and has been stocked artificially, but there is a good range of species, including rhino and even a couple of elephants—although these have to be replaced periodically as a full grown elephant would devastate this small area. Each time they grow too large they are transported and some more babies are brought in!

Recycled elephants

Cross Kopje. Visible from everywhere in town, the kopje sits right on the Mozambique border and is crowned by a massive 10-metre high stone cross, floodlit at night, erected by Colonel Methuen as a memorial to the African soldiers who died in the First World War.

Murahwa's Hill. Another small nature reserve of just one kopje. You will rarely see anything larger than monkeys but there is always a very strong smell of cat, and leopards are known to live here. A short and enjoyable walk. Reached from Jan Smuts Drive.

Museum. Founded in 1957 and moved to the present building in 1964, the museum is small and rather dusty but has an interesting gallery of local history, some live snakes and an aviary. Open 9am to 5pm daily except for Christmas Day and Good Friday. On Aerodrome Rd. PO Box 920, Mutare. Tel: 63630.

Utopia House Museum. Built in 1897, this was the home of Kingsley Fairbridge. It is typical of houses of the period, few of which still survive thanks to the unceasing hard work of the local termites. It has been restored and furnished for the period between 1910 and 1920. Open on Friday afternoons only. On Jason Moyo Drive. Ask for further details through the museum.

Sights in the Surrounding Area
Lake Alexander. The Odzani Dam was built in the 1960s as a reservoir for Umtali and to fuel a small hydro-electric station. It has since also become a local playground and home of the yacht club, with fishing, small boats and picnic areas. 40 km from Mutare, past Penhalonga. Take the Penhalonga Road which turns right off the Harare Road just over Christmas Pass.

La Rochelle. Sir Stephen and Lady Courtauld's home which was left to the nation. The magnificent garden is now maintained by a trust and is open to the public daily from 8am to 5pm. 13 km from town along the Penhalonga Road.

Accommodation
There are no first class hotels in town and few people other than business travellers stay in the centre, generally preferring to use one of the small hotels in the Vumba (see below).

Mid-range hotels.
Manica***: The largest and poshest in town. Perfectly comfortable, very convenient and totally uninspiring. Run by Zimbabwe Sun. Aerodrome Rd. PO Box 27, Mutare. Tel: 64431. Telex: 81106.
Wise Owl Motel**: Low-slung and informal, but pleasant. About 3 km from the centre of town, just off the Harare Road at the foot of Christmas Pass. PO Box 588, Mutare. Tel: 64643.
Christmas Pass Hotel: About 5 km from the centre of town at the top of Christmas Pass. This has had wild swings of fortune and it is difficult to tell when it's going to be fine and when dreadful. OK at present. Tel: 63818.

Budget hotels.
City Centre Hotel: One of the cheapest in town,

and more salubrious now than in the past. 62 Herbert Chitepo Street, Mutare. Tel: 62441.

Camping. The *Municipal Camping and Caravan Site* is 5 km from the centre of town near the top of Christmas Pass. Views and facilities good, but not terribly pretty. PO Box 910, Mutare. Tel: 64412.

There is also a camping and caravan site in *Penhalonga Village*, 17 km from Mutare.

THE VUMBA RANGE

Lie back and
think of
England

A small, gentle range of hills about 28 km south of Mutare, the Vumba are cool, lush, green and enjoyable if unadventurous. People from Mutare tend to treat them as an extension of the town, going up for tea, an evening meal or just for a stroll. The name means 'mist', a singularly apt one for an area that is often shrouded in cloud, but for homesick expatriates, there are rich emerald meadows, apple trees and woodland. Even the climate conspires to make you think you've never left England.

Things to See

Bunga Forest Reserve. An area of natural woodland covering 1558 hectares laid out with a network of paths for walkers. Dark, damp and cool, with a lovely earthy smell. 27 km from Mutare on both sides of the main Vumba Road, which turns off from the Masvingo Road just out of town.

Vumba Botanical Garden. Formerly called the Manchester Gardens, this 200 hectare reserve was purchased for the nation in 1958 and is now run by the National Parks Service. It was originally the property of a family who created a wonderful garden where daffodils and violets grow alongside tree ferns and orchids. 32 km from Mutare along the main Vumba Road.

Burma Valley. This is the other side of the hills from Mutare, where the land suddenly drops about 900 metres to a frost-free valley that is intensively farmed for coffee, cotton and tropical fruit. A 70-km scenic loop road leads through the valley with some spectacular views right across Mozambique. The turn-off is along the Vumba Road, about 2 km past the Impala Arms on the right.

Spectacular
views into
Mozambique

Accommodation
Hotels.

The Inn on the Vumba**: Small, pleasant hotel in the foothills, 8 km from Mutare, just off the Vumba Road. PO Box 524, Mutare. Tel: 60722.

Leopard Rock: Recently redeveloped and very luxurious resort with golf course and casino. About 27 km from Mutare in the Vumba. PO Box 1297, Harare. Tel: Harare 700711. Fax: Harare 704457.

White Horse Inn**: Very small (only 8 rooms), but carefully thought out. Very British, with cream teas and a croquet lawn, but all set against a backdrop of thick forest. The food is reckoned to be some of the best in the area. 17 km from Mutare, off the Vumba Road. PO Box 3193, Paulington, Mutare. Tel: 60325.

Cottages.

Cotswold Heights Chalets: 2 furnished chalets to let. 25 km from Mutare near the Botanical Gardens. PO Box 3101, Mutare. Tel: 2127/3.

Rio de Medaos de Ouro Cottage: Basically furnished cottage to let. 20 km from Mutare. PO Box 719, Mutare. Tel: 60722/2947/2910.

Camping. There is a National Parks camping and caravan site next to the *Botanical Garden*. Access is steep, so be careful if towing a caravan. Post Bag V7472 Mutare. Tel: 212722.

The Naro Moru Store on Woodland Road, Vumba, is within walking distance of the campsite and sells basic foods, stamps, etc.

THE NYANGA RANGE

Zimbabwe's largest range   The Nyanga range is the largest in the country and includes too the highest point in Zimbabwe. Many of the lower slopes are forested with pine, those higher are generally scrubby moorland cracked by a web of streams. Yet these are, on the whole, gentle mountains where it is easy to walk in trainers, and no part is truly inaccessible. The name means 'Place of the Witchdoctor'.

There are two main access roads, one through Old Umtali, branching off the Penhalonga Road, which itself turns off the Harare Road about 8 km from Mutare; the other turning off the Harare Road just north of Rusape. The high mountains are 99 km from Mutare and 275 km from Harare. A car is almost essential as distances are too far to walk unless you have a great deal of time and public transport is virtually non-existent.

Things to See

Rhodes Nyanga National Park. Much of the high ground in the mountains, most of it the personal estate of Cecil Rhodes, has been turned into a National Park covering 33,000 hectares. Mainly an area of superb scenic beauty, there are also some small animals and a wide variety of birds to be seen. There are several small lakes within the park that are all excellent picnic spots and some of which have boats for hire. The lakes and rivers are all stocked with trout from the *trout hatchery* just below the *Mare Dam* (this is open to the public) and at Mare, Rhodes and Udu Dams, you may fish throughout the year. Purdon Dam and Lake Gulliver are open for fishing from October to July and river fishing is allowed between October and May. Artificial flies only. There are also regular guided pony trails bookable through the tourist office near Rhodes Dam, just off the main road through to Nyanga Village. Tel: Nyanga 274.

Nyangwe Fort ('Place of the Leopard') is the best preserved and most accessible of the many thousands of small, short-lived forts built in the mountains over the centuries. Even before the main thrust of the Rozwi invasion in the 18th C, there had been much bickering and raiding between the local tribes and people regularly retired to the mountains to these small enclosures, called matanga epasa or 'underground cattle enclosures' to sit it out with their livestock until the danger was past.

They first built an elliptical wall out from the hillside, about 6 metres in diameter and 2 to 3 metres deep, then partly filled it with rubble to create a well-drained level platform inside. The entrance passage was roofed at a height of about 1.5 metres, and had a small hole in the top which some say was to take a pole connected to the owner's neck rest or pillow, the theory being that anyone trying to get through the narrow entrance at night would knock the pole and wake the sleeper.

Nyangwe is just off the road 2 km before reaching Mare Dam from Rhodes Dam or the Park Warden's Office.

Nyangani. On the eastern limit of the National Park squats the flat-topped, brooding shape of Mount Inyangani, the highest mountain in Zimbabwe at 2592 metres. Legend says it is haunted, a place of bad spirits. It is a legend that dates from an incident many years ago when a father and two children vanished without trace while climbing it. That being said, many people do take the path to the top, a climb that can be done in a couple of hours by anyone who is reasonably fit. There is a loop road leading from Mare Dam to the foot of the path about 8 km away.

Pungwe Falls and Gorge. In the far south of the National Park is one of its most spectacular sights, where the Pungwe River tumbles in the most magnificent of Nyanga's many beautiful waterfalls into a wild, twisting gorge. The falls, and the Pungwe

A hill fort near Nyangwe

View just above them, are reached from the Scenic Road that loops off the main Mutare-Nyanga Road.

Mtarazi Falls and the Honde Valley. Just south of the Pungwe Gorge another small National Park protects the Mtarazi Falls, at 762 metres Zimbabwe's highest waterfall. The narrow stream that tumbles over the cliff vanishes into dense, almost jungle-like woodland. The mountain range ends abruptly here, dropping vertically and dramatically into the Honde Valley. The Honde View, a spectacular panoramic viewpoint, is about a kilometre before you reach the falls. Both are reached off a long, wriggly scenic road that branches off the main road from Mutare to Nyanga Village and loops round to rejoin it near the Park Warden's Office. There is a rudimentary and overgrown footpath leading down the cliff to the valley, but this isn't recommended.

The Honde Valley is reached from the Scenic Road, with a turn-off on the right just after leaving

and highest waterfall

the main road. It is a rich garden area and the main

Tea plantations centre for tea production in the country with over 2000 hectares of tea plantations. From the valley floor you can get an excellent view of the Mtarazi Falls and Mount Nyangani, travel up the last section of the Pungwe Gorge, the giant redwoods meeting over your head and see close-up the strange series of granite pinnacle rocks on the Pungwe-Honde watershed that were visible from the cliff above. There is an old track that loops round and up to the higher ground near Troutbeck, but this is only passable with four-wheel drive.

Connemara and World's View. North of the National Park the mountains again come to an abrupt end as a cliff-like escarpment drops 900 metres to the plains below. There are two viewing points, at World's View and Eagle's View. The crystal clarity of the air makes a dramatic sight even more spectacular as the purple landscape stretches forever beneath your feet. On a clear day it is said that you can see Harare 200 km away. There is a very rough and precipitous footpath leading down into the valley for those with strong heads. Just before you reach the cliff is a series of high, cold mountain streams and lakes, ice-blue water tumbling over lichen-covered rocks. This is Connemara, where quite a few Zimbabweans keep country cottages. To get here, turn right off the Nyanga Village Road towards Troutbeck. Just before you reach the Troutbeck Inn (about 15 km further), turn to your left. The road leads through Connemara to the views, about 5 km from the turn-off.

Van Niekerk and Nyahokwe Ruins. The Nyanga district is covered by the greatest concentration of

Greatest concentration of ancient structures stone-built ruins in the whole of Zimbabwe, with terracing, enclosures and forts over an area of 6500 sq km. The greatest single complex is the Van Niekerk ruins, named after the man who guided archaeologist Randall McIver to the site in 1905.

This is a city which covered over 80 sq km, clustered round three peaks, the most important being Ziwa Mountain (height 1745 metres), called after a 19th C chief, Saziwa. Here on both sides of the Nyangombe River are a mass of terraces, parallel walls and circular enclosures, each thought to have surrounded a group of huts. On the slopes of the mountain a walled path leads to an area which was probably the home of the chief or was a religious sanctuary. The vast amount of stone work, done partly for defence, partly to provide level platforms for housing and agriculture, is very rough and often, to our eyes, illogical, but the site is remarkable well preserved with seats and grinding stones left *in situ*, almost as though the town had been abandoned overnight. Most of the building here is relatively late and short-lived, work of the baRwe tribe, a section of the Karanga people from the 17th to early 19th C.

Just along the road from here are the Nyakhokwe ruins, named after Hokwe, a 19th C chief of the Nyama tribe (part of the Mbire, also a Karanga group). Although this is a much smaller site, it shows almost continuous inhabitation over a very long period, firstly by the Ziwa people until the 11th C, then by the first builders in stone from the 11th to 15th C—probably part of the same migration that saw the arrival of the great builders of Great Zimbabwe. The main stone building period was that of the baRwe from the 16th to 18th C, after which the Nyama people moved into the site, living here until the 19th C.

Stone builders' migration

Little work has yet been done on the Nyanga peoples, so the archaeological record is scanty and probably highly inaccurate. There is a small site museum at Nyahokwe showing the main finds from both these sites.

These two sites are both on a rough circular road leading north from Nyanga Village down the escarpment below World's View. Check before you leave whether it is safe as they are extremely isolated and in an area that has remained a trouble hotspot with strong rumours of Mozambiquan bandits operating freely.

Villages. There are two small villages in the mountains. One is at Juliasdale, near where the roads from Mutare and Harare, via Rusape, link up. The second, Nyanga Village, is just north of the National Park along the main road. Both have garages, stores and post offices. There is also a store near Troutbeck Inn which sells basics.

Accommodation
Upmarket hotels.
Troutbeck Inn***: Only three stars but worthy of more in most peoples' minds. This country house style hotel with chintz covers and a log fire that has burned constantly for over 30 years is one of the best in the country. There is only one set meal per evening, but the food too is probably the best in the country. The hotel has over 600 hectares of land with its own lake, golf course and stables. North of the National Park, near Connemara. Turn right off the main Nyanga Road just before Nyanga village. PO Troutbeck, Mutare. Tel: Nyanga 305. Telex: 81277 ZW. Or book through Zimbabwe Sun Central Reservations Office, Harare (see Appendix).

Montclair Casino Hotel***: This is also luxurious, with its own casino for those in need of a gamble. A pretty building with lovely views, the Montclair is lower down, on the main Nyanga Road just outside Juliasdale. PO Juliasdale. Tel: Juliasdale 4441. Telex: 81272 ZW.

Mid-range hotels.
Rhodes Nyanga*: Set just near Rhodes Dam and the Park Warden's Office, this small hotel was built around Rhodes' own house. Post Bag 8024N, Rusape. Tel: Nyanga 377.

Brondesbury Park***: On the Rusape Road, the Brondesbury Park is some way from the mountains proper. It has recently been taken over and renovated by the Zimbabwe Tourist Development Corporation. Post Bag 8070, Rusape. Tel: Juliasdale 341.

Budget hotels.

Pine Tree Inn: Recently reopened under new management, this small hotel is again a bit far from the mountains proper—about 800 metres off the Rusape Road before you reach Juliasdale. PO Box 1, Juliasdale. Tel: (129) 25916.

Nyanga Holiday Hotel*: Small and fairly basic, not licenced to serve drinks. Off the Nyanga Road, just before you reach Nyanga Village. PO Box 19, Nyanga. Tel: 336.

Self-catering. The National Parks Service operates a large number of chalets at *Mare Dam*, *Rhodes Dam* and *Udu Dam*. They all have their own cooking, bathing and toilet facilities and an attendant is shared between two cottages to do basic cleaning, tidying, etc. For more information or to book, contact the National Parks Central Booking Office, Harare.

There are also a number of private cottages in the area immediately around the National Park, many of which are let for holidays. Ask a local travel agent for details.

Camping.

Mare River Caravan Site: This site is 500 metres west of the Tourist Office on the banks of the Mare River. It has full facilities, but is open to caravans only.

Nyangombe Camping Site: Open to both campers and caravaners and situated 3 km from the Tourist Office on the main Nyanga road. Again there are plenty of facilities.

THE CHIMANIMANI MOUNTAINS

Formidable mountainscape

The scenery in the Chimanimanis changes dramatically yet again, the mountains blue with bare, craggy rock, more formidable than anything seen elsewhere in the country, yet still breathtakingly beautiful. Further south still the land drops into the dry, red, dusty plains of the low veld, a world of scrubby bush and baobabs, and vast, intensively irrigated cotton plantations.

Chimanimani Village

The southern road from Mutare is probably the worst of the main through roads in the country. Although it is tarred, it is narrow, fairly badly potholed in places and should be driven with caution. It is a 150-km drive to Chimanimani Village.

Originally named Melsetter in 1892 by founder Thomas Moodie after his ancestral home in the Orkneys, the village has never been anything other than a very small but nevertheless charming settlement used as a centre by local farmers and as a base for tourists. It does have all the basic facilities you may need, and even a country club.

Bridal Veil Falls, 4.5 km from the village, is a very pretty waterfall on the Nyahodi River. It is a narrow fall that drops almost vertically down a 50 metre cliff into a small pool in a wooded glade. There is an **eland sanctuary** just outside Chimanimani Village.

Chimanimani National Park

The National Park is a narrow strip of land about 50 km long, pressed up against the Mozambique border. Here is a true feeling of mountainous isolation, though the mountains are not in reality as high as those in Nyanga, with a top altitude of 2437 metres. The raw granite and quartzite peaks plunge into a series of savage gorges supporting a varied

211

and unlikely flora that includes cedar trees and orchids.

Unlike the other parks in the country, there hasn't been even the most rudimentary development here. There are no roads within the boundaries, only a sparse network of small footpaths. A rough gravel road leads the 19 km from Chimanimani Village to the foot of the mountains where there are a car park, information office and small base camp with ablution facilities. There is a mountain refuge hut on the west bank of the Bundi River.

None of the walks is too far and can be attempted by anyone reasonably fit, but care should be taken as the weather is very changeable and thick mist can descend without warning. Also take care not to cross the border into Mozambique.

To contact the park: Post Bag 2063, Chimanimani. Tel: 0-3322.

Undeveloped wilderness

To Chipinge and South

Chipinge can be reached by driving 50 km through the mountains south from Chimanimani Village. But if you are approaching the Eastern Highlands from the west, that is from the direction of Masvingo, you will drive over the **Birchenough Bridge** where the Masvingo and Mutare roads meet. This impressive arch of steel is the largest single span suspension bridge in southern Africa.

First settled in 1893, **Chipinge** is a rather dusty agricultural town whose architecture places a great deal of emphasis on corrugated iron. It is however the second largest town in Manicaland.

Chirinda Forest Reserve, near Mount Selinda and 32 km south of Chipinge, is one of the last remaining areas of what was probably once a massive primaeval forest. Fed by the low damp clouds that often cover this area, there are a number of unique botanical species. The reserve covers 949 hectares and includes some massive trees, most of them red mahogany and ironwood. The country's largest tree, a red mahogany that stands 66 metres high and has a girth of 15 metres is here.

Accommodation
Hotels.

Chimanimani**: Comfortable and in a very pretty surroundings, this is also the social centre of Chimanimani Village. PO Box 5, Chimanimani. Tel: Chimanimani 511.

Chipinge: In the centre of Chipinge, this is not a place of great beauty, but clean and comfortable enough in a spartan sort of way. PO Box 27, Chipinge. Tel: Chipinge 2226.

Camping. There is a small camping and caravan site with full facilities in Chimanimani Village. Ask at the hotel for details.

In Chimanimani National Park the small base camp with ablution facilities is available on a first-come first-serve basis for groups of up to six people. Ask the Park Warden. Otherwise, camping is unrestricted and free within the park as long as due care is taken.

SECTION 6: APPENDIX

Language: Useful Words and Phrases

Old and New Place Names

Customs Allowances

Some Zimbabwe Embassies and Tourist Offices Abroad

Some Foreign Embassies in Zimbabwe

Tour Companies, Car Hire and Accommodation Central Booking Offices in Zimbabwe

LANGUAGE: USEFUL WORDS AND PHRASES

English is the official language and you will rarely, if ever, find anyone who speaks no English at all. There are several tribal languages and dialects, but by far the most widely spoken are Shona and Ndebele. They are not written languages in origin and there are still discrepancies in spelling as people use a phonetic approximation. There are words for numbers, days of the week, time, etc, but you will never hear them used as the English equivalent is just slotted into the conversation.

ENGLISH	SHONA	NDEBELE
Basics		
How are you?	Makadii zvenyu?	Linjani/Kunjani?
Good/fine/well	Ndiripo zvangu	Sikhona/Ngiyaphila/ Siyaphila
Bad	Handisi kunsa zvak- anaka	Angiphilanga kuhle
Thank you	Ndatenda/Mazvita	Ngiyabonga/Siyabonga kakalu
Please	Ndapota	Uxolo
Goodbye	Chisarai zvakanaka	Lisale sesihamba/ Lisale kuhle
Welcome	Titambirei	Siyalemukela
Danger	Ngozi	Ingozi
Friend	Shamwari	Mngane/Umngane
Sorry	Ndine urombo	Uxolo
Excuse me	Pamusoroi	Uxolo/Ngixolela
Good morning	Mangwanani	Livuke njani
Good afternoon	Masikati	Litshonile
Good evening	Manheru	Litshone njani
Where?	Kupi?	Ngaphi?
When?	Rini?	Nini?
How?	Sei/Nei?	Njani?
Time		
What time is it?	Dzava nguvai?	Yisikhati bani?
Now	Zvino	Khathesi
Morning	Mangwanani	Ekuseni
Afternoon	Masikati	Emeni yantambama
Evening	Manheru	Ntambama
Today	Nhasi	Lamhla

Yesterday	Nezuro	Izolo
Tomorrow	Mangwana	Kusasa
Time/hour	Nguva	Isikhati
Night	Usiku	Ebusuku
Day	Kwakachena	Emini

Numbers

One	Potsi	Okukodwa
Two	Piri	Okubili
Three	Tatu	Okuthathu
Four	Ina	Okune
Five	Shanu	Okuyisihlanu
Six	Tanhatu	Okuyisithupha
Seven	Nomwe	Okuyisikhombisa
Eight	Tsere	Okuyisitshiyangalo mbili
Nine	Pfumbamwe	Okuyisitshiyangalo lunye
Ten	Gumi	Okuli tshumi

Days of the week

Sunday	Svondon	Ngesonto
Monday	Muvhoro	Umvolo/Ngumvulo
Tuesday	Chipiri	Ngolwesibili
Wednesday	Chitatu	Ngolwesithathu
Thursday	China	Ngolwesine
Friday	Chishanu	Ngolwesihlanu
Saturday	Mugovera	Ngesabatha

Game animals

Leopard(s)	Mbada	Ingwe
Rhinoceros	Chipembere	Ubhejane
Buffalo(s)	Nyati	Inyathi
Lion(s)	Shumba	Isilwane/Ngwenyama
Elephant(s)	Nzou	Indhlovo
Baboon/monkey	Gudo (Bveni/Tsoko)	Indwangu/Inkawu
Zebra	Mbizi	Idube
Impala	Mhara	Impala
Giraffe	Swiza	Intundla
Hyena	Bere	Impisi
Warthog	Njiri	Ingulube yeganga
Hippo(s)	Mvuu	Imvubu

People

Man/men	Murume/Varume	Indoda/Amadoda
Woman/women	Mukadzi/Vakadzi	Umfazi/Abafazi
Mister/Sir	Changamire	Umnimzana
Child/children	Mwana/Vana	Umtwana/Abantwana
Old man/men	Murume/Varume/ Vakuru	Ixegu/Amazegu
Girl(s)	Musikana/Vasikana	Inkazana/Amankanaza

Madam	Mudzimai/Madzimai	Umfana/Abafana
Eating and shopping		
How much?	I marii?	Yimalini?
Expensive (very)	Zvinodhura	Kuyadula
Shop	Chitoro	Isitolo
Money	Mari	Imali
Another/more	Rimwe	Futhi/Okunye
Beer	Doro/Whawha	Utshwala
Bread	Chingwa	Isinkwa
Eggs	Mazai	Amaqanda
Enough	Zvakwana	Kwenele
Fish	Hove	Inhlanzi
Fruit(s)	Muchero/michero	Izithelo
Ice/cold	Chando/hunoton-hora	Okuqandayo
Meat	Nyama	Inyama
Milk	Mukaka	Ucago
Potatoes	Matapiri	Amagwili
Rice (cooked)	Mupinga waka-bikwa	Irice ephikiweyo
Salt	Munyu	Isaudo
Small, little/big	Diki/Shoma/Guru	Okuncane/Ncinyane
Vegetables	Muriwo	Umbhida/Imbhida
Hot	Kupisa	Kuyatshisa
Water	Mvura	Amanzi

OLD AND NEW PLACE NAMES

After independence, many place names were changed, either restoring a more accurate spelling of a local word, or giving a native name in place of a colonial one.

Old	New
Balla Balla	Mbalabala
Belingwe	Mberengwa
Chipinga	Chipinge
Dett	Dete
Enkeldoorn	Chivhu
Essexvale	Esigodini
Fort Victoria	Masvingo
Gatooma	Kadoma
Gwelo	Gweru
Hartley	Chegutu
Inyanga	Nyanga
Inyazura	Nyazura
Mangula	Mhangura
Marandellas	Marondera
Mashaba	Mashava
Matopos	Matobo
Mazoe	Mazowe
Melsetter	Chimanimani
Mrewa	Murewa
Mtoko	Mutoko
Mtoroshanga	Mutorashanga
Nkai	Nkayi
Nuanetsi	Mwenezi
Que Que	Kwe Kwe
Salisbury	Harare
Selukwe	Shurugwi
Shabani	Zvishavane
Sinoia	Chinhoyi
Sipolio	Guruve
Somabula	Somabhula
Tjolotjo	Tsholotsho
Umniati	Munyati

Umtali	Mutare
Umvukwee	Mvurwi
Umvuma	Mvuma
Vila Salassar	Saago
Wankie	Hwange

CUSTOMS ALLOWANCES

The following can be imported duty free into Zimbabwe. All visitors must fill in a Customs Declaration Form on arrival.

(1) Personal

Items temporarily imported for personal use such as clothing, toiletries and make-up.

One watch, and other personal equipment such as hair dryer, calculator, camera etc.

(2) Gift allowance

New goods to a value of not more than Z$1000. This may not be used more than once in 30 days, for trade purposes, or if you have only been out of the country for a day. Families travelling together can pool their allowance.

(3) If over 18, you can take in 5 litres of alcohol, including not more than 2 litres of spirits. There is no limit on tobacco, but cigarettes are cheaper in Zimbabwe than even duty-frees in Europe, so importing isn't worthwhile.

(4) Currency: No more than Z$100 may be taken out in local currency. There is no restriction on the import or export of foreign currency, as long as it has been declared on arrival and a certificate of importation obtained.

SOME ZIMBABWE EMBASSIES AND TOURIST OFFICES

Embassies

Belgium: 21–22 Av des Arts, B-1040 Brussels. Tel: 02-230 8551/35/67.

Botswana: IGI Building, PO Box 1232, Gaborone. Tel: 314495.

Canada: 332 Somerset St West, Ottawa, Ontario K2P 0J9. Tel: (613) 237 4388/9/4.

France: 5 Rue de Tilsitt, Paris 75008. Tel: 47 63 48 31.

German Federal Republic: Villichgasse 7, 5300 Bonn 2. Tel: (0228) 356 071.

Kenya: 6th Floor, ICDC Building, Mamlaka Road, PO Box 30806, Nairobi. Tel: 721 071.

Sweden: Sveavägen 9–11 10390 Stockholm. Tel: 08–2446695.

Tanzania: Plot 408, Longido St, Upango, Dar es Salaam. Tel: 34896.

United Kingdom: Zimbabwe House, 429 The Strand, London WC2R 0SA. Tel: 071-836 7755.

USA: 1608 New Hampshire Ave NW, Washington DC. Tel: (202) 332 7100.

Zambia: 4th Floor, Ulendo House, Cairo Road, PO Box 33491, Lusaka. Tel: 229 382.

Tourist Offices

Head Office: Tourism House, 105 Jason Moyo Ave, Harare. PO Box 8052, Causeway, Harare. Tel: 793666/7/8/9 and 706511/2/3. Fax: 793669.

German Federal Republic: Steinweg 9, D-6000 Frankfurt am Main 1. Tel: 069-294 042/3. Telex: 413849 ZIMBA-D.

South Africa: Upper Shopping Level, Carlton Centre, Johnnesburg. PO Box 9398, Johannesburg 2000. Tel: 331 3137. Telex: 4-88561 SA.

United Kingdom: at the Zimbabwe High Commission (see under Embassies).

USA: Suite 1905, Rockefeller Center, 1270 Ave of the Americas/16th Ave, New York, NY 10020. Tel: 212-307 6565/8. Telex: 261038 ZTDR UR.

SOME FOREIGN EMBASSIES IN ZIMBABWE

Australia: 4th Flr, Karigamombe Centre, Samora Machel Ave, Harare. Tel: 794591.

Austria: New Shell House, 30 Samora Machel Ave, Harare. Tel: 702921/2.

Belgium: 4th Flr, Tanganyika House, Union Ave, Harare. Tel: 793306/7.

Botswana: 22 Philips Ave, Belgravia, Harare. Tel: 729551/2/3.

Canada: 14242 Straker Ave, Gunhill, Harare. Tel: 735071.

Denmark: 1st Flr, UDC Centre, 59 Union Ave, Harare. Tel: 790398/9.

Finland: 3rd Flr, Karigamombe Centre, Samora Machel Ave, Harare. Tel: 704499.

France: Ranelagh Road, Highlands, Harare. Tel: 48096/8.

German Federal Republic: 14 Samora Machel Ave, Harare. Tel: 731955.

Greece: 8 Deary Ave, Belgravia, Harare. Tel: 723747.

Italy: 7 Bartholomew Close, Greendale, Harare. Tel: 47279.

Kenya: 95 Park Lane, Harare. Tel: 790847.

Netherlands: 47 Enterprise Road, Highlands, Harare. Tel: 731428.

Norway: 92 Josiah Chinamano Rd, Harare. Tel: 792419.

Portugal: 10 Samora Machel Ave, Harare. Tel: 725107.

South Africa: Trade Mission, Temple Bar House, Baker Ave, Harare. Tel: 707901.

Spain: 16 Philips Ave, Belgravia, Harare. Tel: 738681.

Sweden: 7th Flr, Pegasus House, Samora Machel Ave, Harare. Tel: 790651.

Switzerland: 9 Lanark Road, Belgravia, Harare. Tel: 703997.

Tanzania: 23 Baines Ave/Blakiston St, Harare. Tel: 724173.

United Kingdom: Stanley House, Jason Moyo Ave, Harare. Tel: 793781.

USA: Arax House, 172 Herbert Chitepo Ave, Harare. Tel: 794521.

Zambia: Zambia House, Union Ave, Harare. Tel: 790851/2.

TOUR COMPANIES, CAR HIRE AND ACCOMMODATION CENTRAL BOOKING OFFICES IN ZIMBABWE

Main Zimbabwean Tour Companies and Agents

Buffalo Safaris and Zambezi Canoeing: PO Box 113, Kariba. Tel: Kariba 2645. Telex: 41281 HANVAL ZW.

Bush Tracks Safaris: PO Box 64, Victoria Falls. Tel: 341.

Garth Thompson Safari Consultants: Room 410, Monomotapa Hotel, PO Box 5826, Harare. Tel: 795287. Telex: 2364 ZW.

Manica Travel Services: Travel Centre, Jason Moyo Ave. PO Box 776, Harare. Tel: 703421. Telex: 24316 ZW.

Safari Par Excellence: 2 Trustee House, 55 Samora Machel Ave, Harare. Po Box 5920, Harare. Tel: 720527/700911. Telex: 22171 SFLINK.

United Touring Company: Travel Centre, Jason Moyo Ave, Harare. PO Box 2914, Harare. Tel: 793701. Telex: 2173 ZW.

Shearwater Adventures: 5th Floor, Karigamombe Centre, Julius Nyerere Way, (PO Box 3961), Harare. Tel: 735712. Telex: 26391 ZW

Zambezi Trails: Suite 318, Meikles Hotel, Third Street, (PO Box 825). Marare. Tel: 723719/705040. Telex: 6063 ZW. Fax: 735716.

The Zimbabwe Tourist Board publishes a booklet with the names and addresses of all tour operators within Zimbabwe. Specialist operators in each district are included in the relevant area chapter.

Car Hire

Avis:

Harare: 5 Samora Machel Ave. Tel: 720351/704191. Telex; 4156.

Harare Airport: Tel: 50121 (also for after hours use).

Bulawayo: 99 Robert Mugabe Way/10th Ave. Tel: 68571/61306. Telex: 3613.

Bulawayo Airport: Tel: 26657.

Kariba: Oasis Service Station. Tel: 555.
Victoria Falls: Livingstone Way/Mallet Drive. Tel: 532. Telex: 3593.

Europcar/Echo Car Hire:
Harare: 19 Samora Michel Ave (next to Jameson Hotel), (PO Box 3430, Harare). Tel: 706484/5/9, 702221/2/3 (after hours: 84860/4, 723953). Telex: 4641.
Harare Sheraton: Pennefather Ave. Tel: 729771/700080.
Bulawayo: Bulawayo Sun Hotel, 10th Ave, (PO Box 2320, Bulawayo). Tel: 67925/74157 (after hours: 64243). Telex: 3361.

Hertz:
Harare: United House, Park Avenue. Tel: 792791/793701/727209. Telex: 4741.
Harare Airport: Tel: 50320 (also after hours no).
Meikles Hotel, Harare: Tel: 793701.
Monomotapa Hotel, Harare: Tel: 793701.
Jameson Hotel, Harare: Tel: 794641.
46 Samora Machel Ave, Harare: Tel: 704915/793701.
Bulawayo: Cnr George Silundika St/14th Ave. Tel: 74701/61402. Telex: 3384.
Bulawayo Sun Hotel: Tel: 61402.
Bulawayo Airport: Tel: 27177 (also after hours no.)
Victoria Falls: CABS Building. Tel: 267/8. Telex: 3221.
Victoria Falls Airport: Tel: 32522.
Mutare: Publicity Bureau. Tel: 64711.
Kariba: Cutty Sark Hotel. Tel: 420.
Lake View Inn, Kariba: Tel: 427.
Caribbea Bay Hotel, Kariba.
Masvingo: Founders House, Robert Mugabe St. Tel: 2131. Telex: 3499.
Hwange: Hwange Safari Lodge. Tel: Dete 24. Telex: 3479.
Chiredze: Lowveld Travel. Tel: 295. Telex: 3491.

Central Booking Offices
Cresta Hotels: P/Bag AY2 Amby, Harare. Tel: 703131. Telex: 26453 ZW.

Goodwood Hotels: PO Box 1490, Harare. Tel: 705081. Telex: 24164 ZW. Fax: 707599.

National Parks Service: National Botanical Gardens, Sandringham Drive, Harare. PO Box 8151, Causeway, Harare. Tel: 706077.

Zimbabwe Sun: Travel Centre, Jason Moyo Ave, PO Box 8221, Harare. Tel: 736644. Fax: 734739.

PO Box 654, Bulawayo. Tel: 60101. Telex: 3242.

UK Tour Operators with Trips into Zimbabwe

Abercrombie and Kent: Sloane Square House, Holbein Place, London SW1. Tel: 071-730 9600.

Safari Par Excellence: 27–31 Jerdan Place, London SW6 1BE. Tel: 071–381 5229.

United Touring International: Paramount House, 71–5 Uxbridge Rd, Ealing Broadway, London W5 5SL. Tel: 081–566 1660.

Africa Travel Centre: 4 Medway Court, Leigh St, London WC1H 9QX. Tel: 071-387 1211.

Safari Consultants Ltd: 83 Gloucester Place, London W1H 3PG. Tel: 071-486 4774/935 8996.

Worldwide Journeys and Expeditions: 8 Comeragh Rd, London W14 9HP. Tel: 071–381 8638.

A great many more include Zimbabwe in multi-country itineraries. For a full list, contact the Zimbabwe Tourist Office.

INDEX

Accommodation   25–28, 110–112, 120, 126, 131, 137–38, 150–151, 153–155, 162–163, 180–181, 182, 191–192, 200–201, 203, 209–210, 213, 226–227
African National Congress   82, 84, 91, 95, 96
Agama   43
Air travel   see Travel by . . .
Antbear   50
Antelope   43, 50, 57–59, 119, 171, 178, 211
Arab traders   65–66
Australopithicenes   63

Baboons   51, 143
Banks   33
Bantu   65, 70, 82, 171
Baobabtree   146, 211
Basketry   36
Beer   30
Bees   45
Beit Bridge   10, 81, 157, 175
Bilharzia   15
Biltong   29
Binga   136
Birchenough Bridge   81, 212
Birds   59–62, 118, 119, 152, 164, 199, 204
Boerevoes   29
Boomslang   44, 48
Borders, international   10, 130, 144, 195
Braaivleis   28, 32, 151
British South Africa Company   73, 76, 78, 81, 158, 164, 172, 197
Bulawayo   10, 19, 20, 22, 23, 32, 37, 42, 70, 71, 76, 78, 84, 94, 95, 97, 109, 152, 157–165, 166, 172, 186
Buffalo   51, 52, 127
Bumi Hills   136, 137, 138
Buses
   airport   23, 106, 128, 149, 157, 177
   inter-city   23, 107, 157, 177, 194, 198
   local   24, 107, 158, 177, 182, 194, 197
Bushbaby   43, 51
Bushbuck   57, 58, 143
Bushmen   63, 65, 171, 172, 173
Bushpig   52–53

Camping   27–28, 112, 120, 122, 125, 126, 131, 137, 138, 150–151, 153–155, 159, 163, 174, 178, 180–181, 191–192, 201, 203, 210, 212, 213

Camping gas   see Fuel
Car hire   19, 22, 107, 128, 149, 157, 177, 197, 225–226
Caracal   55
Caravanning   see Camping
Carvings   38–39, 133,
Casinos   33, 134, 149, 209
Cats   53–55
Cave paintings   65, 164, 171–172, 173
Chameleon   43
Changamire   67, 68, 70
Chapungu Kraal   115
Charter   73, 79
Cheetah   54–55
Chimanimani   211–213
Chinhoyi
   caves   18, 121–122
   town   121–122
Chipinge   26, 212–213
Chirundu   10
Chizarira   17
Chongalolo   43
Civet   55
Climate   12–14, 194–195
Clothing   14–15, 35,
Clubs   32
Cobra   45, 46, 47–48
Colonisation   71–78
Communications   18
Crane, crowned   59–60
Credit cards   11
Cricket   32
Crime   41
Crochet   37
Crocodile   57, 135, 146–147
Customs allowances   220

Dance   31, 148–149
Departure tax   11
Dhlo Dhlo   163
Diesel   see Fuel
Doctors   16
Drink   30–31, 34
Duiker   58

Eagle, fish   60
Eastern Highlands   13, 16, 19, 42, 48, 51, 193–213
Egret, cattle   59
Egyptian cobra   47
Eland   58, 211

Electricity   33, 102, 124, 128–130, 200
Elephant   28, 42, 50, 55–56, 127, 174,
                180, 191, 199
Embassies   221–224
Emeralds   37
English explorers   70–75
Epworth balancing rocks   115
Ewanrigg Botanical Gardens   16, 18,
                          115, 116

Farming   101, 175, 196, 211
Federation   83–84
Film   see photography
Fishing   119, 125, 127, 134–135, 138,
                151, 169, 178, 180, 204
Food   28–29, 35
Football   31
Forestry   101
Fort Victoria   see Masvingo
Fothergill Island   138
Fox, bat-eared   53
Fuel   21, 33, 125, 137, 153, 191
Fura Mountain   67, 68, 69, 185

Gaboon viper   47
Game viewing   49–50, 119, 126–127,
136, 138, 145, 148, 152–155, 163, 165, 169,
                174, 178, 182, 199
Gecko   43
Gemstones   37–38
Genet   50, 55
Giraffe   52
Gokomere people   65
Gold   67–68, 69, 70, 71, 78, 101, 185
Golf   32
Gonarezhou   17, 191–192
Government   81
Great Zimbabwe   6, 65, 67, 68, 71, 163,
            166, 167, 177, 178, 179, 181–190
Guinea fowl   60
Gweru   19, 22, 92, 157, 175

Harare   10, 16, 18, 19, 20, 22, 23, 25, 29,
32, 33, 40, 78, 84, 94, 96, 106–115, 121,
125, 128, 136, 151, 157, 158, 175, 204, see
                        also Salisbury
Health   15, 35, 46–49
Heroes Acre   117
Heron, grey   60
Hippopotamus   57, 134
History   6, 63–96, 107–109, 121, 124,
125, 128–130, 139–141, 144, 145, 158, 163,
164, 166–168, 175, 182–185, 197–205, 207–
                        209, 211
Hitchhiking   24, 152, 194
Homo sapiens (Boskopoid)   63

Honde Valley   205–207
Hoopoes   62
Hornbills   60
Hornets   44–45
Hotels   25–26, 29, 31, 32, 33, 110–111,
120, 122, 131, 137, 138, 149–150, 155, 162,
180, 182, 200–201, 203, 209–210, 226–227
Hwange   13, 16, 17, 19, 29,147, 152–155
Hyena, spotted   53

Impala   28, 58
Industry   102
Inoculations   15
Ivory   39, 71

Jackal   44, 53
Jameson, Leander Starr 75, 78, 108, 173

Kalahari   13, 16
Kalanga   103
Karanga   65, 66, 103, 185, 187, 208
Kariba
    dam   10, 124, 128–138
    town   19, 22, 23, 33, 37, 130–135
Kazuma Pan   17
Kazangula   10
Khami Ruins   166–168
Kingfishers   62
Kingsley Fairbridge   198, 199–200
Kudu   59
Kuruman   71
Kyle   18, 177, 179–181, 182

Land apportionment   76, 78, 79, 82, 88,
                          93, 98
Language   215–217
Larvon Bird Gardens   117
Leguaan   180
Leopard   43, 54, 143, 199
Limpopo   10, 67, 70, 81, 124
Lion   53–54, 117
Livingstone, David   69, 70, 140–141
Lobengula   70, 71, 72, 73, 75, 76, 109,
                      158, 164, 166
Locust   43

Magosina peoples   63
Makishi dancers   148–149
Malaria   15, 44
Mamba   44, 46, 48
Mambo   67
Mana Pools   17, 125–127, 147
Manicaland   75–76, 98, 193–213
Manyika   68, 103
Mambo   67
Mana Pools   17, 125–127, 147

Manicaland 75–76, 98, 193–213
Manyika 68, 103
Maps 4–5, 106, 116, 132, 142, 170, 176, 186, 195
Masks 38, 148
Mashona see Shona
Mashonaland 71, 75, 76, 79, 98, 105–122, 158
Masvingo 75, 98, 157, 175–178, 182, 212
Matabele see Ndebele
Matabeleland 13, 41, 71, 75, 76, 79, 97, 98, 156–174
Matobo (Matopos) 18, 78, 169–174
Matusadona 17, 136–137, 138
Mauch, Karl 71
Mazowe 67
Mcllwaine, lake 18, 119–120
Medicines 35
Metric conversion table 34
Midlands 98
Military action 89, 90, 92, 94, 95
Minerals 67, 71, 78, 101–102
Missionaries 68, 69, 71, 140, 158, 163, 168, 178
Money 11–12
Monkeys 50–51, 171, 199
Monomotapa see Mwene Mutapa
Mtarazi Falla 206
Mugabe, Robert 91, 92, 95, 96, 97, 98
Music 32, 148–149
Mushandike 18
Mutare 7, 10, 13, 20, 22, 75, 78, 175, 194–201, 204, 209, 211, 212
Muzorewa, Abel 89, 91, 93, 95, 96
Mwari 66, 67
Mwene Mutapa 67, 68, 69, 70, 75, 185
Mzilikaze 70, 71, 169
Mzilikaze's roller 60–61

National Archives 113, 159
National Parks 16–18, 28, 119, 122, 125–127, 136, 147, 150–151, 152–155, 169–174, 178, 179–181, 191–192, 202, 203, 204–210, 211–213
Ndebele 70, 76, 78, 91, 97, 103, 158, 166, 167, 173, 215–217
Ngezi 18
Night ape 51
Nikomo, Joshua 84, 85, 86, 91, 95, 96, 97
Nyama 28
Nyanga 26, 33, 65, 69, 194, 204–210, 211
Nyangani 205, 207
Nyati 71

Opening hours 33

Operation Noah 131–133, 138
Organising 18–19, 109–110
Ostrich 29, 61
Otto Beit Bridge 81

Paraffin see Fuel
Petrol see Fuel
Photography 36, 40–41
Pioneers 75, 175, 177
Place names 218–219
Plumtree 10
Poachers 42
Portuguese 68–70, 75, 78, 163, 167
Post 18, 33
Pottery 36–37
Prehistory 63–67
Public holidays 35
Puff adder 44, 46–47
Pungwe 205–206
Python 49

Rabies 15, 44
Rail see Travel by . . .
Reedbuck 59
Rhinoceros 42, 56, 57, 119, 180, 199
Rhodes, Cecil 72, 75, 76, 78, 109, 144, 158, 164, 169, 172–173, 204
Rhodesia 76
Rhodesian Front 86
Rinkal 48
Roads see Travel by . . .
Rondaavels see Self-catering
Rozwi 66–67, 103, 167, 205
Rudd Concession 73, 75, 158
Rusape 26, 209

Sabi River 81
Sable 59
Sadza 28
Salisbury 73, 75, 108 see also Harare
Samango monkeys 50–51
Sanctions 87, 88
Sandawana 37
Scrub hairs 50, 143
Sculpture 39
Sebakwe 18
Secretary bird 61
Security 41–42, 97
Segregation 81–82, 83, 85, 86, 88, 93
Self-catering 27, 120, 126, 137, 153–155, 180–181, 191–192, 203, 210
Serum, snakebite 46
Serval 55
Shangaan Patrol 173
Shangaan people 103, 148–149

Shona 65, 66–67, 68, 70, 78, 91, 92, 103,
        215–217
Shopping   33, 35–39
Sithole, Ndabaningi 86, 91, 92, 93, 95
Smith, Ian   87, 91, 92, 93
Snakes   43, 44, 45–49, 147, 199
Souvenirs   36–39
Spiders   43, 44
Spirits   30
Spitting cobra   47
Sport   32, 119
Starling, glossy   61
Swimming   32, 119, 134

Taxis   22, 107, 128, 157, 197
Telephones   18
Telex   18
Tennis   32
Theatre   32
Tiger Bay   138
Time   35
Tipping   31
Tobacco Auction Rooms   114
Tonga   103, 128, 133
Tour Companies   225
Tourism   102
Tourist Offices   221–222
Trains   see Travel by Rail
Travel
  air 10, 19–20, 106, 126, 128, 136, 137,
        138, 152, 157, 175–176, 194,
  boat 125, 127, 128, 134, 136, 137, 138,
        147–148, 180, 191, 204
  rail 20, 72, 78, 106, 108, 144, 152, 157,
        161, 172, 194, 197, 198
  road 10, 20–24, 106, 119, 125, 128,
        136, 137, 138, 152–153, 157, 175, 191,
        194, 198, 204

Tsetse fly   45

UDI   85, 87, 89, 95
Umtali   see Mutare

Venda   103
Vervet monkeys   50–51,
Victoria Falls 10, 19, 20, 23, 26, 29, 33,
38, 40, 42, 78, 83, 124, 134, 135, 136,
                139–151, 157
Vine snake   48–49
Vipers   46, 47
Visas   10–11
Voting 79, 81, 83, 84, 85, 88, 89, 93,
                95–96, 97
Vultures   62
Vumba   18, 69, 200, 202–203

Warthog   28, 52
Water, drinking   16
Waterbuck   59
Weaver birds   61
Wild dog   53
Wildebeeste   51, 178
Wildlife 6, 41, 43–62, 131–133, 136–138,
    147, 152–155, 163, 164, 174, 178, 199
Wine   30–31

Zambezi
  national park   18
  river   10, 67, 68, 71, 81, 123–151
ZANU   86, 91, 92, 93
ZANU (PF)   95, 97
ZAPU   86, 91, 92
Zebra   50, 52
Zimbabwe birds   185–186
Zimbabwe, Great see Great Zimbabwe
Zulus   70, 172, 173

NOTES